First hundred words in Polish

Heather Amery

Illustrated by Stephen Cartwright

Translation and pronunciation guide by
Ivona Abramian and Neil Bowdler

Designed by Mike Olley and Jan McCafferty

There is a little yellow duck to find in every picture.

Salon The living room

Tata
Daddy

Mama
Mummy

chłopiec
boy

iewczyna

girl

niemowlę

baby

pies

dog

kot

cat

Ubranie Clothes

buty
shoes

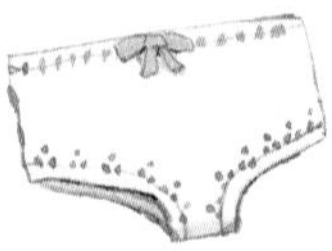

majtki
pants

sweter
jumper

kamizelka

vest

spodnie

trousers

T-shirt

t-shirt

skarpetki

socks

Kuchnia The kitchen

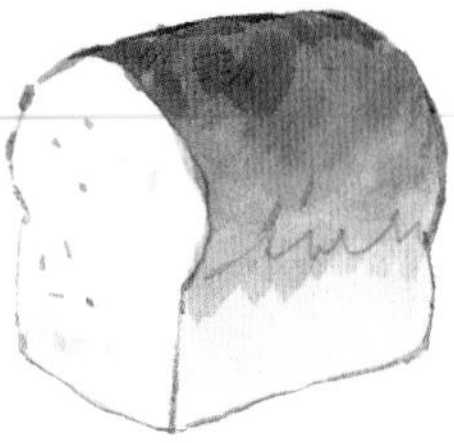

chleb
bread

mleko
milk

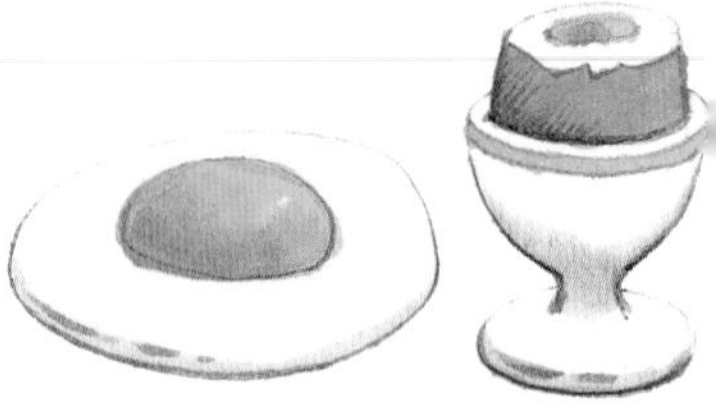

jajka
eggs

jabłko

apple

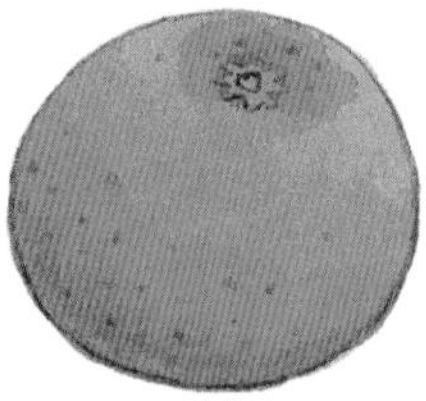

pomarańcza

orange

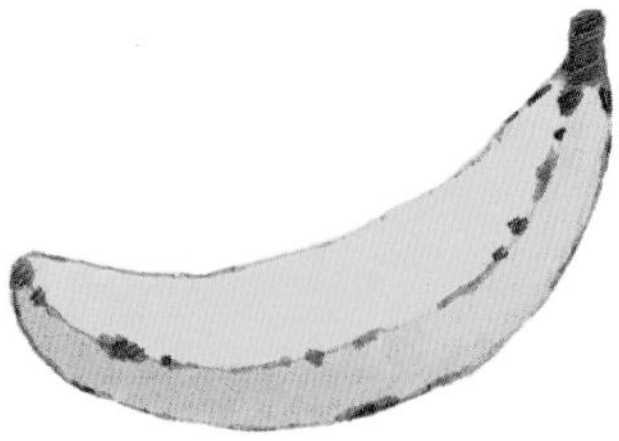

banan

banana

Zmywanie naczyń Washing up

stół
table

krzesło
chair

talerz
plate

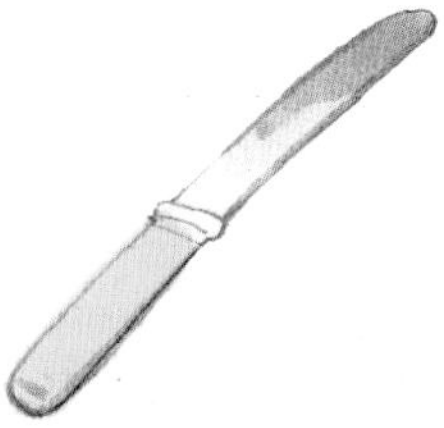

nóż
knife

widelec
fork

łyżka
spoon

filiżanka
cup

Zabawki Toys

koń

horse

owca

sheep

krowa

cow

kura
hen

świnia
pig

kolejka
train

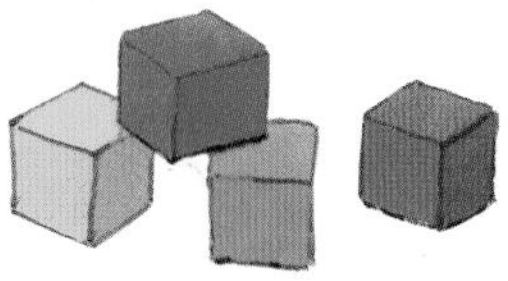

cegły
blocks

Z wizytą On a visit

babcia
Granny

dziadek
Grandpa

pantofle
slippers

płaszcz

coat

sukienka

dress

czapka

hat

Park The park

drzewo
tree

kwiat
flower

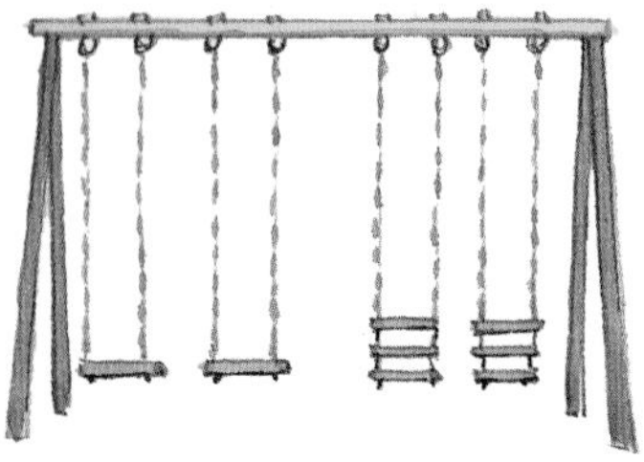

huśtawki
swings

piłka
ball

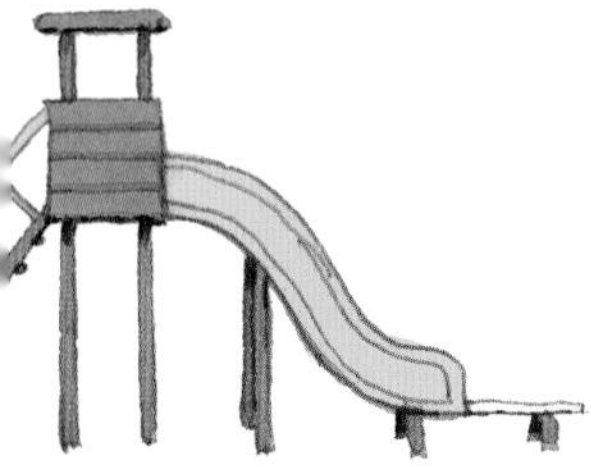

eżdżalnia
slide

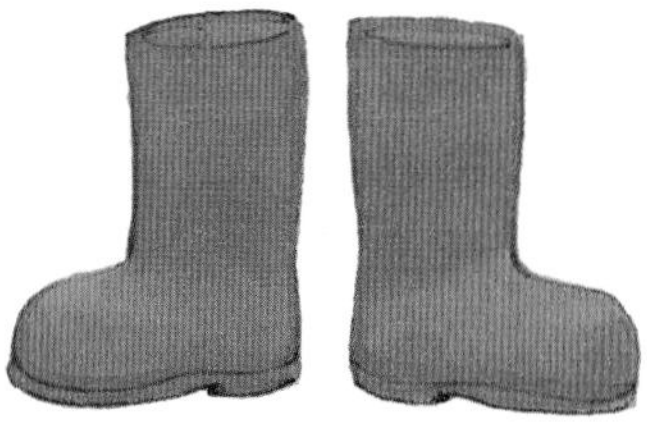

kalosze
wellington boots

ptak
bird

łódź
boat

Ulica The street

samochód
car

rower
bicycle

samolot
plane

ciężarówka
truck

autobus
bus

dom
house

Przyjęcie The party

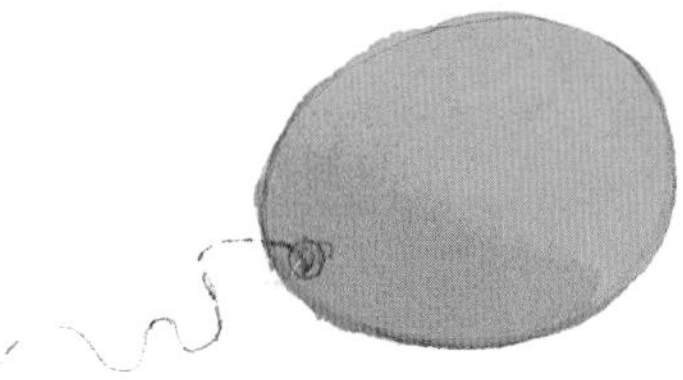

balon
balloon

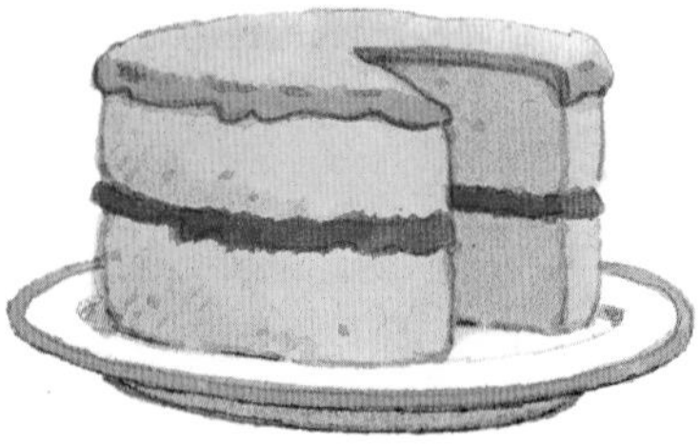

ciasto
cake

zegar
clock

lody

ice cream

ryba

fish

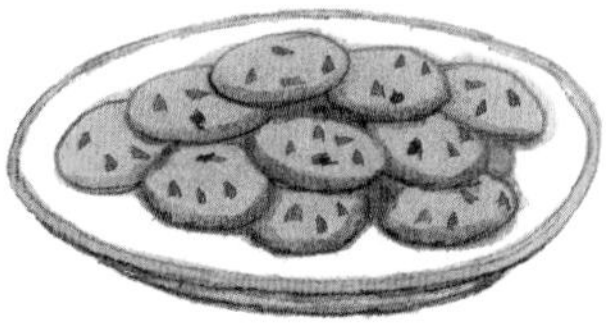

herbatniki

biscuits

cukierki

sweets

Pływalnia The swimming pool

ramię
arm

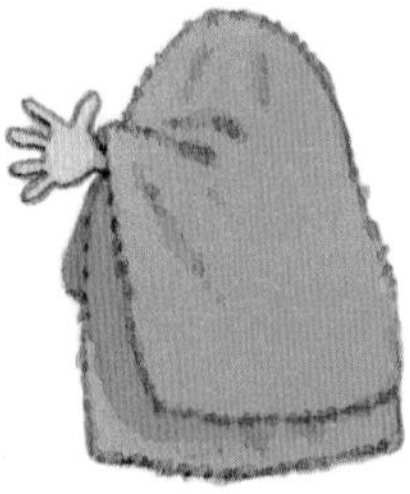

ręka
hand

noga
leg

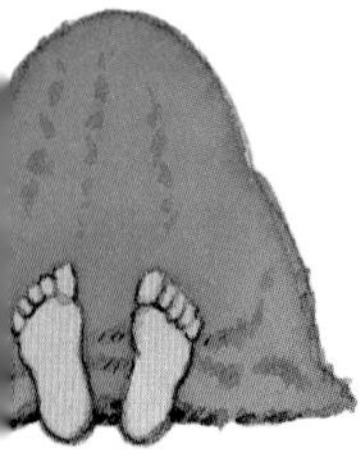

topy
feet

palce u nóg
toes

głowa
head

pośladki
bottom

Przebieralnia The changing room

usta
mouth

oczy
eyes

uszy
ears

nos

nose

włosy

hair

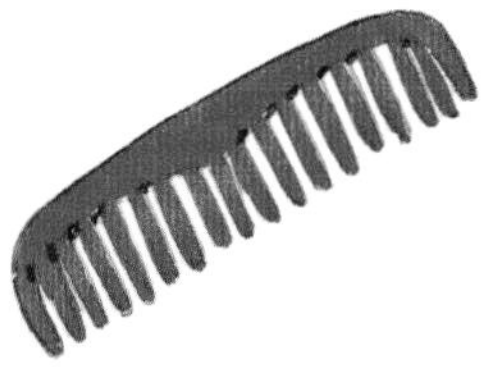

grzebień

comb

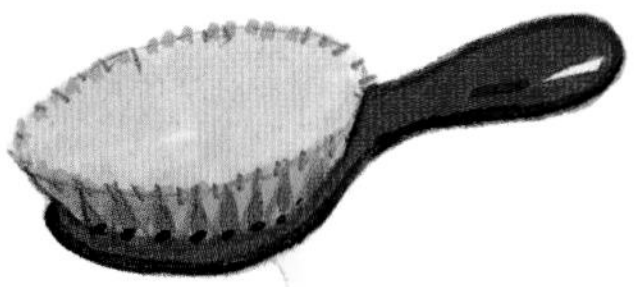

szczotka do włosów

brush

Sklep The shop

czerwony
red

niebieski
blue

zielony
green

żółty
yellow

różowy
pink

biały
white

czarny
black

Łazienka The bathroom

mydło

soap

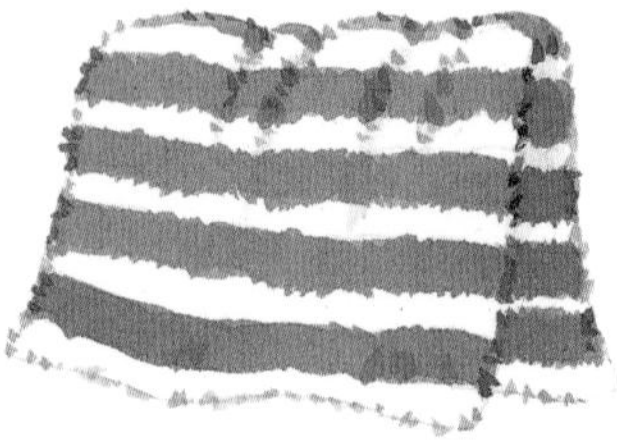

ręcznik

towel

toaleta

toilet

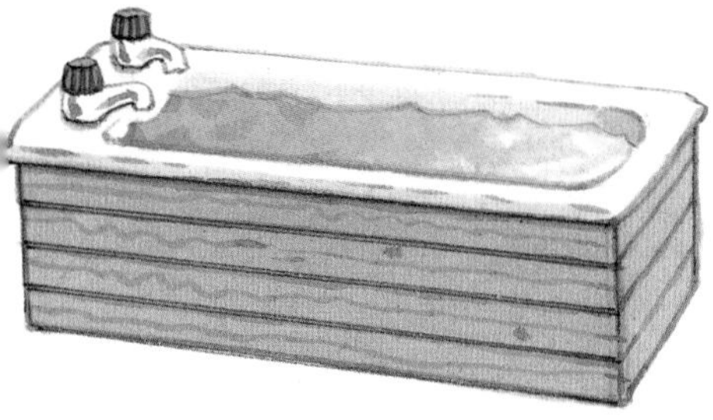

wanna

bath

brzuch

tummy

kaczka

duck

Sypialnia The bedroom

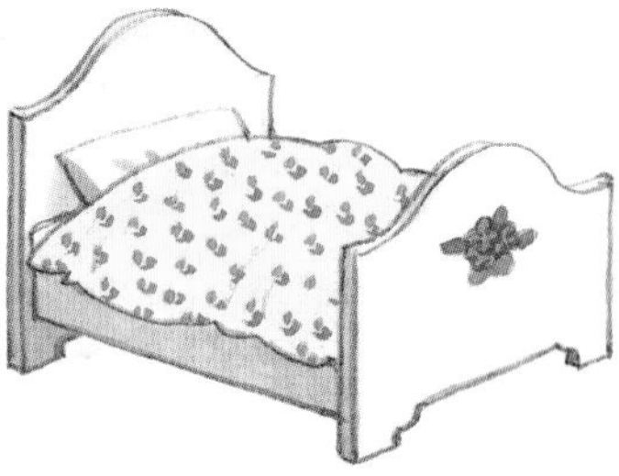

łóżko
bed

lampa
lamp

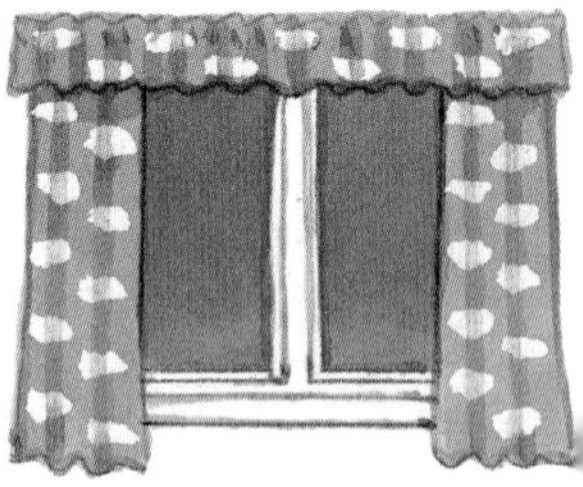

okno
window

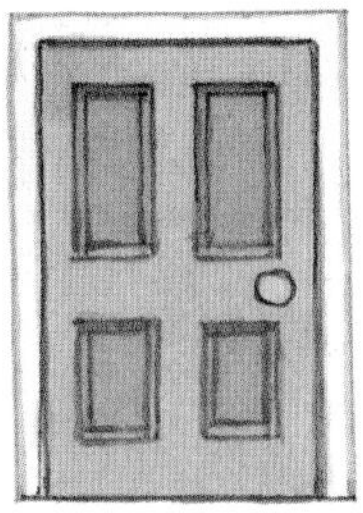

drzwi
door

książka
book

lalka
doll

pluszowy miś
teddy

Match the words to the pictures

banan
ciasto
czapka
jabłko
jajko
kaczka
kalosze
kamizelka
kolejka
kot
krowa
książka
lalka
lampa
lody

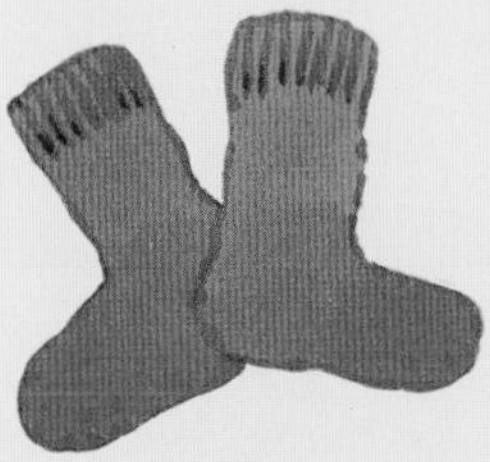

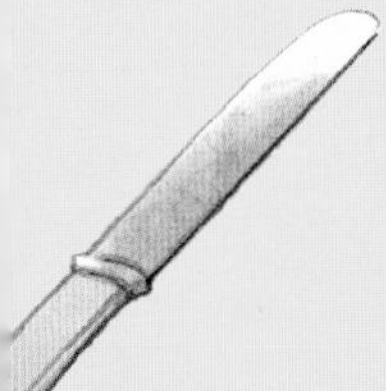

mleko

nóż

okno

pies

piłka

pluszowy miś

pomarańcza

ryba

samochód

skarpetki

stół

sweter

świnia

widelec

zegar

Liczby Numbers

1 jeden
one

2 dwa
two

3 trzy
three

4 cztery
four

5 pięć
five

1 jeden
one

2 dwa
two

3 trzy
three

4 cztery
four

5 pięć
five

ord list

his alphabetical list of all the words
ne pictures, the Polish word comes
, next is a guide to saying the word,
then there is the English translation.
guide may look strange or funny, but
try to read the words as if they were
lish. Most Polish words have a part
: you stress, or say louder (like the
y" part of the English word "today").
you know which part of each word
should stress, it is shown in letters
this in the pronunciation guide.

It will help you to say the words in Polish correctly if you remember these rules:

a in the guide is like the *a* in c*a*t

i in the guide is a sound in between the *i* in ch*i*p and the *ee* in ch*ee*se

ike in the guide rhymes with b*ike*

ow in the guide rhymes with c*ow*

y is like the *y* in *y*et, except at the end of a word where it is like the *y* in cit*y*

zh is like the *s* in trea*s*ure

obus	*ow**toe**bus*	bus
cia	***bab**cha*	Granny
on	***bal**on*	balloon
an	***ban**an*	banana
y	***byow**y*	white
uch	***bzhookh***	tummy
y	***boot**y*	shoes
ły	***tseg**wy*	blocks
eb	***hleb***	bread
opiec	***hwop**yets*	boy
sto	***chast**o*	cake
arówka	*chenzha**roof**ka*	truck
ierki	*tsoo**kyer**ki*	sweets
pka	***chap**ka*	hat
rny	***char**ny*	black
rwony	*cher**von**y*	red
ery	***chter**y*	four
n	***dom***	house
ewo	***dzhev**o*	tree
wi	***dzhvee***	door
a	***dva***	two
adek	***jad**ek*	Grandpa
ewczyna	*jef**chin**na*	girl
anka	*feelee**zhan**ka*	cup
wa	***gwov**a*	head
ebień	***gzheb**yen*	comb

herbatniki	*herbat**neek**i*	biscuits
huśtawki	*hoos**tav**ki*	swings
jabłko	***yabw**ko*	apple
jajka	***yike**-a*	eggs
jajko	***yike**-o*	egg
jeden	***yed**en*	one
kaczka	***kach**ka*	duck
kalosze	*ka**losh**e*	wellington boots
kamizelka	*kami**zel**ka*	vest
kolejka	*ko**ley**ka*	train
koń	***konn***	horse
kot	***kot***	cat
krowa	***krov**a*	cow
krzesło	***ksheswoe***	chair
książka	***kshonzh**ka*	book
kuchnia	***kooh**nya*	kitchen
kura	***koor**a*	hen
kwiat	***kvyat***	flower
lalka	***lal**ka*	doll
lampa	***lam**pa*	lamp
liczby	***leech**by*	numbers
lody	***lod**y*	ice cream
łazienka	*wa**zhen**ka*	bathroom
łódź	***woodj***	boat
łóżko	***woozh**ko*	bed
łyżka	***wizh**ka*	spoon

majtki	***might**ki*	pants
Mama	***ma**ma*	Mummy
mleko	***mlek**o*	milk
mydło	***mid**wo*	soap
niebieski	***nyeb**yeski*	blue
niemowlę	*nye**mov**le*	baby
noga	***nog**a*	leg
nos	***nos***	nose
nóż	***noozh***	knife
oczy	***och**y*	eyes
okno	***ok**no*	window
owca	***ov**tsa*	sheep
palce u nóg	***pal**tse oo **noog***	toes
pantofle	*pan**tof**le*	slippers
park	***park***	park
pies	***pyess***	dog
pięć	***pyench***	five
piłka	***peew**ka*	ball
pluszowy miś	*ploo**shov**y **meesh***	teddy
płaszcz	***pwashch***	coat
pływalnia	*pwy**val**nia*	swimming pool
pomarańcza	*pomar**ran**cha*	orange
pośladki	*posh**lad**ki*	bottom
przebieralnia	*pshebye**ral**nya*	changing room
przyjęcie	*pshi**yen**che*	party
ptak	***ptak***	bird
ramię	***ram**ye*	arm
ręcznik	***rench**neek*	towel
ręka	***ren**ka*	hand
rower	***rov**er*	bicycle
różowy	*roo**zhov**y*	pink
ryba	***ribb**a*	fish

salon	***sal**on*	living r
samochód	***sam**ohood*	car
samolot	***sam**olot*	plane
skarpetki	*skar**pet**ki*	socks
sklep	***sklep***	shop
spodnie	***spod**nye*	trouser
stopy	***stop**y*	feet
stół	***stoo***	table
sukienka	*soo**kyen**ka*	dress
sweter	***sfet**er*	jumper
sypialnia	*sip**yal**nya*	bedroo
szczotka do włosów	***shchot**ka do **vwos**oof*	hairbru
świnia	***shveen**ya*	pig
talerz	***tal**ezh*	plate
Tata	***ta**ta*	Daddy
toaleta	*toal**et**a*	toilet
trzy	***tshy***	three
T-shirt	***T**-shirt*	t-shirt
ubranie	*oo**bran**ye*	clothes
ulica	*oo**leet**sa*	street
usta	***oos**ta*	mouth
uszy	***oosh**y*	ears
wanna	***van**na*	bath
widelec	*vee**del**ets*	fork
włosy	***vwos**y*	hair
zabawki	*za**bav**ki*	toys
zegar	***zeg**ar*	clock
zielony	***zhel**ony*	green
zjeżdżalnia	*zyezh**jal**nya*	slide
zmywanie naczyń	*zmi**van**ye **na**chinn*	washin up
z wizytą	*z**veez**iton*	on a vi
żółty	***zhoot**y*	yellow

First published in 2008 by Usborne Publishing Ltd, Usborne House, 83-85 Saffron Hill, London EC1N 8RT, England. www.usborne.com

Soft Workouts

Low Impact Exercise

FITNESS, HEALTH & NUTRITION

Soft Workouts

Low Impact Exercise

TIME LIFE

by the Editors of Time-Life Books

CONSULTANTS FOR THIS BOOK

Robert M. Otto, Ph.D., is Director of the Human Performance Laboratory at Adelphi University, Garden City, N.Y. He is a member of the American College of Sports Medicine's Preventive and Rehabilitative Exercise Program Committee and of the Fitness Instructor Subcommittee, which is responsible for the development of Dance Exercise Certification.

Ann Grandjean, Ed.D., is Associate Director of the Swanson Center for Nutrition, Omaha, Neb.; chief nutrition consultant to the U.S. Olympic Committee; and an instructor in the Sports Medicine Program, Orthopedic Surgery Department, University of Nebraska Medical Center.

Myron Winick, M.D., is the R.R. Williams Professor of Nutrition, Professor of Pediatrics, Director of the Institute of Human Nutrition, and Director of the Center for Nutrition, Genetics and Human Development at Columbia University College of Physicians and Surgeons. He has served on the Food and Nutrition Board of the National Academy of Sciences and is the author of many books, including *Your Personalized Health Profile.*

The following consultants helped design the exercise sequences in this book:

Risa Friedman has a master's degree in dance education and is certified in health fitness by the American College of Sports Medicine, the International Dance Exercise Association and the Laban-Bartenieff Institute of Movement Studies. She has taught anatomy/kinesiology, movement analysis, therapeutic exercise, exercise physiology, and fitness and dance at New York University and the State University of New York, among other institutions. She is an exercise physiologist in private practice in San Diego, California, and is Program Director of the Fitness Specialist Certification Program at Marymount Manhattan College in New York City.

Jane Katz, Ed.D., is a Professor of Health and Physical Education, Bronx Community College of the City University of New York. An All-American Masters swimmer and synchronized swimming champion, Katz holds several World and National Masters swimming records. She is also a recipient of the National Fitness Leaders Award, given by the U.S. Jaycees and the President's Council on Physical Fitness.

Judy L. Marriott is a Certified Movement Analyst with the Laban-Bartenieff Institute of Movement Studies and an exercise trainer. She is also a professional dancer and has performed with several companies nationally and internationally.

Jean Ann Scharpf, M.A., is an exercise physiologist; Professor of Physical Education at Suffolk County Community College, Sheldon, N.Y.; and is certified as an exercise test technologist by the American College of Sports Medicine. As president of Shaping Routines; Inc., a fitness consulting firm, Scharpf is an aerobic and fitness instructor for educational, corporate and training workshops.

This edition published in 2004
by the Caxton Publishing Group
20 Bloomsbury Street, London WC1B 3JH

Under license from Time-Life Books BV.

Cover Design: Open Door Limited, Rutland UK

Title: Soft Workouts

ISBN: 1 84447 161 6

This book is not intended as a substitute for the advice of a physician. Readers who have or suspect they may have specific medical problems, especially those involving muscles and joints, should consult a physician before beginning any programme of strenuous physical exercise.

CONTENTS

CHAPTER ONE

Soft Fitness

Reducing the impact of exercise to prevent injury, maintain health benefits and increase enjoyment

As exercise programmes proliferate and research on them gains in sophistication, so the standards of what makes exercise beneficial are changing. The notion that a workout should be painful or exhausting — that it should "burn" — has lost its validity, and a growing number of doctors and physiologists affirm that more moderate forms of exercise, which fall under the umbrella term "soft workouts", can improve fitness. One reason for this move towards gentler exercise is the rising incidence of injuries associated with some popular activities, particularly aerobic dance and running. Making soft workouts a part of your fitness programme can be beneficial, since fewer stressful movements mean less risk of injuries. But equally important, such exercises are accessible to people who are intimidated by — or who have tried and given up — highly strenuous regimens. A crucial aspect of any exercise is that it be performed regularly. In providing a series of safe, effective and enjoyable routines, this book will help you towards that goal.

What is a soft workout?

Any exercise that minimizes the stress that is placed on the body's musculoskeletal system can be considered a soft workout. Also known as low-impact or low-percussive exercise, this type of workout provides an alternative to such exercise as high-impact aerobic dance and running — two activities that are considered high in the stress they place on the body, and yet are also among the most popular forms of exercise, with millions of people participating in one or the other. In both running and traditional aerobic dance, you are airborne briefly, and the force of landing and taking off can jar your muscles, joints and ligaments, resulting in soreness or injury. Soft workouts dissipate such force by ultilizing movements that enable you to keep one foot on the ground, and by offering such low-impact environments or surfaces as an exercise mat or a swimming pool.

What types of injuries do soft workouts help you avoid?

The injuries that committed exercisers tend to sustain are not usually of the obvious, acute kind, such as a sprained wrist or a fractured ankle. Rather, people who exercise regularly are more prone to stress, or overuse, injuries, which occur over time as a result of repeated strains on joints, bones and muscles. Typically, a stress injury occurs when the body is subjected to shock or impact while running or jumping, and the body's machinery does not absorb the force effectively. This can occur for a variety of reasons, including poor technique, inadequate equipment and biomechanical abnormalities — such as being flat-footed — that cause forces of exercise to be unevenly distributed through the musculoskeletal system. Though they are often less traumatic than acute injuries, stress injuries can take the form of a wide range of debilitating conditions, from the inflammation of muscles and tendons to muscle tears or hairline fractures in bones.

The rate of stress injuries varies for different activities. As many as 20 per cent of joggers have to stop running for at least a week during each year because of running-related injuries. One in 10 runners suffers an injury each year — usually involving the knees, legs, hips or feet — that requires medical attention. A poll of aerobic dance teachers found that 75 per cent of them, as well as 43 per cent of their students, had suffered injuries as a result of their workouts.

For other activities whose movements produce less impact, injury rates are comparatively lower. Even swimmers can sustain stress injuries to the shoulder, however, and weight lifters, who neither jump nor run, are nonetheless prone to stress injuries. In order to lessen the risk of these injuries, anyone who exercises should take such preventive steps as warming up and cooling down adequately, as well as increasing the intensity and frequency of workouts gradually. In addition, making soft workouts a part of your fitness programme can be beneficial, since they minimize or eliminate the movements that create the greatest stress. Furthermore, low-impact routines also tend

The Forces of Walking and Running

Both running and walking entail two phases: propulsion, or push-off, and landing. In running, the propulsive phase must exert enough force to propel the body off the ground; researchers now suspect that this phase can place as much stress on the foot as landing. Surprisingly, the landing phase of brisk walking can, depending on heel placement, be almost as stressful as that of running. However, the propulsive force is two to three times less in walking, since the body does not have to be launched into the air. This lesser force is what contributes significantly to the low-impact, low-injury quality of walking.

to raise your heart rate more gradually than high-impact exercises do; as a result, you are less likely to feel out of breath or prematurely fatigued if you are embarking on an exercise programme.

Is "soft workout" simply another term for low-impact aerobic dance?
By no means. Certainly low-impact aerobic dance is a popular and effective option for a soft workout. Approximately 70 per cent of aerobic dance teachers who are members of the International Dance-Exercise Association have reported that they offer low-impact aerobic classes to help participants avoid injuries. In these classes, dancers typically have at least one foot on the floor at all times and move their arms constantly — swinging, doing biceps curls, overhead arm presses and so on. These movements help elevate the heart rate and promote aerobic activity that conditions the cardiovascular system. The aerobic dance routine in Chapter Two meets both of these criteria.

Many other types of exercise regimens besides low-impact aerobic movement are considered soft workouts. Fitness walking, which is perhaps the fastest-growing form of exercise in the United States, is

How Workouts Compare

A low-impact exercise such as walking can provide the fitness benefits of high-impact routines such as running without the risks. Two separate studies recorded fitness gains and injuries when groups of sedentary middle-aged women embarked on both low and high-impact exercise programmes. The women in the first study were on a jogging programme, and nearly a third of them developed injuries *(above)*, mostly to the knee and leg. There were no injuries in the second study *(above, right)*, which involved brisk walking, water aerobics and other low-impact routines. The two groups achieved roughly the same improvement in VO_2 max, a measure of how efficiently your body uses oxygen during intense exercise.

inherently low in impact and has a very low injury rate. Whereas both feet leave the ground during a running stride, you always have one foot on the ground when you walk. A section in Chapter Two shows you how to turn walking into a fitness exercise.

Other kinds of soft workouts — such as the routines in Chapter Three, which are performed in water — rely on the cushioning effect of the exercise medium to absorb the shock of movement. Another form of low-impact exercise consists of dancelike movement routines based on principles of kinesiology, the study of how the human body moves. Such routines, which are demonstrated in Chapter Four, can strengthen and tone muscles without undue jarring or strain.

Aren't soft workouts mainly for people who are injured or badly out of shape?

A number of soft workout routines are based on fitness programmes developed for people who were recovering from injuries or who had some other condition — such as pregnancy or obesity — that kept them from participating in more taxing forms of exercise. As a result, soft exercises are accessible to almost anyone, regardless of the participant's physical condition. At the same time, many highly fit people have taken to softening their workouts as a means of injury prevention. Committed exercise enthusiasts who do not want to give up their high-impact programmes are finding that they can integrate soft workouts into their usual routines and obtain the benefits of both. For example, researchers have found that running injuries increase in direct proportion to how often you run and how far you run. A runner concerned with the possibility of being hurt and forced to lay off exercise might choose, therefore, to run three days a week rather than five and to walk, do water workouts or other low-impact aerobics on the other two days. Such a regimen minimizes the risk of injury while maintaining fitness and an active lifestyle. Even professional athletes are taking advantage of low-impact routines: a number of coaches report adding water-based workouts to their teams' training regimens.

Highly trained women may find it especially valuable to alternate soft and hard workouts. Research has shown that strenuous exercise can produce undesirable hormonal changes. One report on female runners found that as many as half of all competitive runners have irregular menstrual cycles, and some actually stop menstruating. Some experts attribute this to lowered levels of the female hormone oestrogen, which can frequently lead to temporary infertility, and lowered calcium levels, which can sometimes cause a loss of bone tissue in the spine. These problems can be halted by cutting back the level of strenuous exercise.

But can soft workouts really exercise your heart intensely enough to be aerobic and improve your endurance?

Building cardiovascular endurance requires improving your oxygen consumption, or aerobic capacity, as this element of fitness is also known. Basically, oxygen consumption is the amount of oxygen that you can extract from the air and transport to working muscles for energy production. How much oxygen you consume is largely dependent on the efficiency of your cardiovascular system. For an exercise to affect oxygen consumption, it must employ large muscle groups such as the legs and arms, and it must be continuous, in order to keep the demand for oxygen high.

Much of the research associated with the aerobic aspect of soft workouts has centred on walking — and virtually all of it shows that rapid walking can produce cardiovascular benefits in most people regardless of their level of fitness. In one study of 343 people spanning the ages of 30 to 69, fast walking enabled nearly all of the women and about two thirds of the men to reach their target heart rates. A person's target heart rate is a percentage of his or her maximum heart rate; it is one indicator that the heart is pumping hard enough during a workout — and that the workout itself is intense enough to be beneficial. As a person gets fitter, he or she must work harder to raise the heart rate because the heart is pumping more efficiently.

Can walking improve your mood? Psychologists tested the reactions of 79 subjects to three types of walking. One group was asked to take a three-minute stroll with a natural gait. The second walked with long strides, swinging their arms and gazing straight ahead. The third group was told to shuffle their feet with eyes cast downwards. The walkers in the first two groups reported an elevated mood, while the shufflers said they felt depressed and tired. The researchers concluded that walking vigorously can help brighten your mood if you are feeling down.

In order to see whether walking could continue to provide effective exercise as fitness levels increased, the same researchers also investigated whether a fitter population could obtain the same results. The outcome of this study — illustrated on page 15 — convinced them that walking can indeed build endurance and produce aerobic conditioning provided that the walkers keep to a pace commensurate with their fitness levels. And in a six-month study of middle-aged women who walked 3 kilometres a day, four days a week, the subjects managed to attain aerobic and muscular improvements comparable to those of a traditional aerobic dance programme.

A good deal of research is now being conducted into whether other types of low-impact workouts can also produce adequate cardiovascular benefits. The data accumulated thus far indicate that they can indeed. For example, one study compared the results of a group of 25 subjects who were required to perform both high-impact and low-impact aerobic dance routines. Although the women's consumption of oxygen rose 28 per cent during the high-impact session, the heart-rate response during both sessions was nearly the same — the pulses that were recorded during the high-impact session averaged only 8 per cent higher than those in the low-impact session. The researchers concluded that although the high-impact routine provided a more intense workout, the low-impact programme also provided an aerobic training stimulus — and that in fact it met the aerobic exercise guidelines set by the American College of Sports Medicine.

What other health benefits do soft workouts provide?

Like all forms of endurance exercise, soft workouts that exercise your heart and lungs can also help tone the skeletal muscles, especially those of the legs, hips, buttocks and abdomen. They have the ability to improve circulation and lung capacity, and can lower elevated blood pressure and reduce psychological stress. Also, several studies suggest that weight-bearing exercises such as walking — that is, exercises that place mechanical stresses on the bone — can strengthen bone composition and slow down osteoporosis, a disease that is characterized by thinning and weakening of the bones.

What is perhaps the most impressive long-term benefit was revealed in a recent study of 35 male postal workers who had been walking an average of 40 kilometres a week for 15 to 28 years. The researchers found that this exercise had a beneficial effect on the subjects' cholesterol levels. The men, aged 36 to 58, had higher than average levels of HDLs, the "good" type of cholesterol-carrying lipoproteins that transport fats out of the bloodstream and thereby reduce the risk of heart disease. The link between long-term walking and increased HDL levels held up even after other factors — including age, leisure activities and alcohol consumption — were taken into consideration. Such a finding is significant because many sports physiologists have reported that, to increase HDL levels significantly, you need to run or perform some other intense aerobic exercise. This study appears to indicate that long-term, low-intensity exercise that is done regularly may provide the same benefit.

Can you achieve any fitness benefits from low-impact activities that do not qualify as complete workouts?

The health improvements that aerobic exercise can provide — lower blood pressure, greater cardiac efficiency, a sense of well-being, more energy, among others — can come only from sustained, regular exercise. But a long-term study conducted by the University of Minnesota in the United States showed that a moderate level of activity does have clear-cut advantages over a sedentary lifestyle. The subjects in the study were men at high risk from heart disease, and researchers found that men who engaged daily in such activities as gardening, dancing, home exercise and other so-called moderate exercise reduced the risk of a fatal heart attack by as much as one third over a seven-year period. Even for people who are not in a high-risk group, activities such as bowling, golf and even doing domestic chores are a positive step towards better health.

Can you lose weight doing soft workouts?

Any exercise that burns calories will help you lose weight, and soft workouts are no exception. A number of studies support the view that soft routines are efficient calorie burners. For example, when 15 sedentary women between the ages of 35 and 64 undertook a 10-week programme of low-impact aerobic dance, their body fat decreased by an average of 2.5 per cent — without controlled dieting. In fact, many studies have shown walking to be an excellent aid to weight control.

However, one researcher notes that you may have to work out for a longer time to burn calories as effectively as those who are exercising more strenuously. In walking research, for example, physiologists have found that moderately brisk walking burns 0.7 calories per kilogram of body weight per kilometre, while running burns 1 calorie. Roughly speaking, that means that you have to walk 1.5 kilometres to get the same caloric expenditure as running for 1 kilometre.

Can a mini-trampoline provide an effective workout?

Rebounding activity on a trampoline, which allows you to run and bounce with or without upper body movement, has been touted as a way to develop cardiovascular endurance; however, there is little evidence thus far to support the claim. Studies have shown minimal increases in aerobic fitness and no change in body composition in programmes lasting from eight to 12 weeks. Other studies show no changes in HDL cholesterol levels.

Experts also acknowledge that a well-trained person will find it hard to reach his or her target heart rate by rebounding on a trampoline. The unconditioned individual can accomplish this goal, but with continued exercising the target heart rate will become more and more difficult to attain. One study did reveal some change in body weight — an average 12 per cent decrease in overweight women. However, it is not uncommon for overweight individuals initially to lose some weight in most exercise programmes, and there is no evidence that this weight would stay off if rebounding was the only exercise they performed persistently. Also, rebounding is not injury free; there have been reports of painful, inflamed tendons associated with the bouncing.

What can movement routines add to a fitness programme?
Movement routines are designed to improve body mechanics, the way you utilize and move your body. They accomplish this by focusing on basic manoeuvres — such as rolling over or rising from a sitting to a standing position — that make you conscious of all the muscles that contribute to performing these actions. This body awareness, in turn, helps you to move effectively by building balance and co-ordination. The routines are extremely low in impact, and many of them incorporate stretching movements that will help to increase your flexibility, a further safeguard against injury.

Are water workouts as effective an exercise as swimming?
Swimming has long been praised as perhaps the single best form of exercise. It builds cardiovascular endurance, develops muscle strength and has a low injury rate. Water workouts are not intended to replace swimming, but they do offer the variety that length swimming lacks, and they can be done by non-swimmers or by anyone whose strokes are not efficient enough to enable him or her to swim lengths.

Research also suggests that water workouts can be an effective and efficient aerobic conditioner. One study of college athletes working out in the water found that they were able to maintain their target heart rates and oxygen consumption during exercise sessions lasting up to 46 minutes. Another study compared target heart rates and other fitness measurements of 14 subjects who did walking and running tests on land and in the water. In the walking segments, their heart rates in the water were elevated about 8 per cent above the rates recorded on land. In the running segments, the heart rates were about equal in both tests — probably because of the difficulty of maintaining a brisk pace in water. In addition, one researcher found that the greater resistance of water as compared to air creates an increased energy requirement of about 34 per cent. As a result, you burn a third more calories performing an exercise in the water than you would performing exactly the same exercise at the same pace on land.

Can you do water workouts and other soft routines while you are recovering from an injury?
Water has long been used for physiotherapy and rehabilitation, and today more and more athletes and exercisers are taking advantage of

Hitting the Target Heart Rate

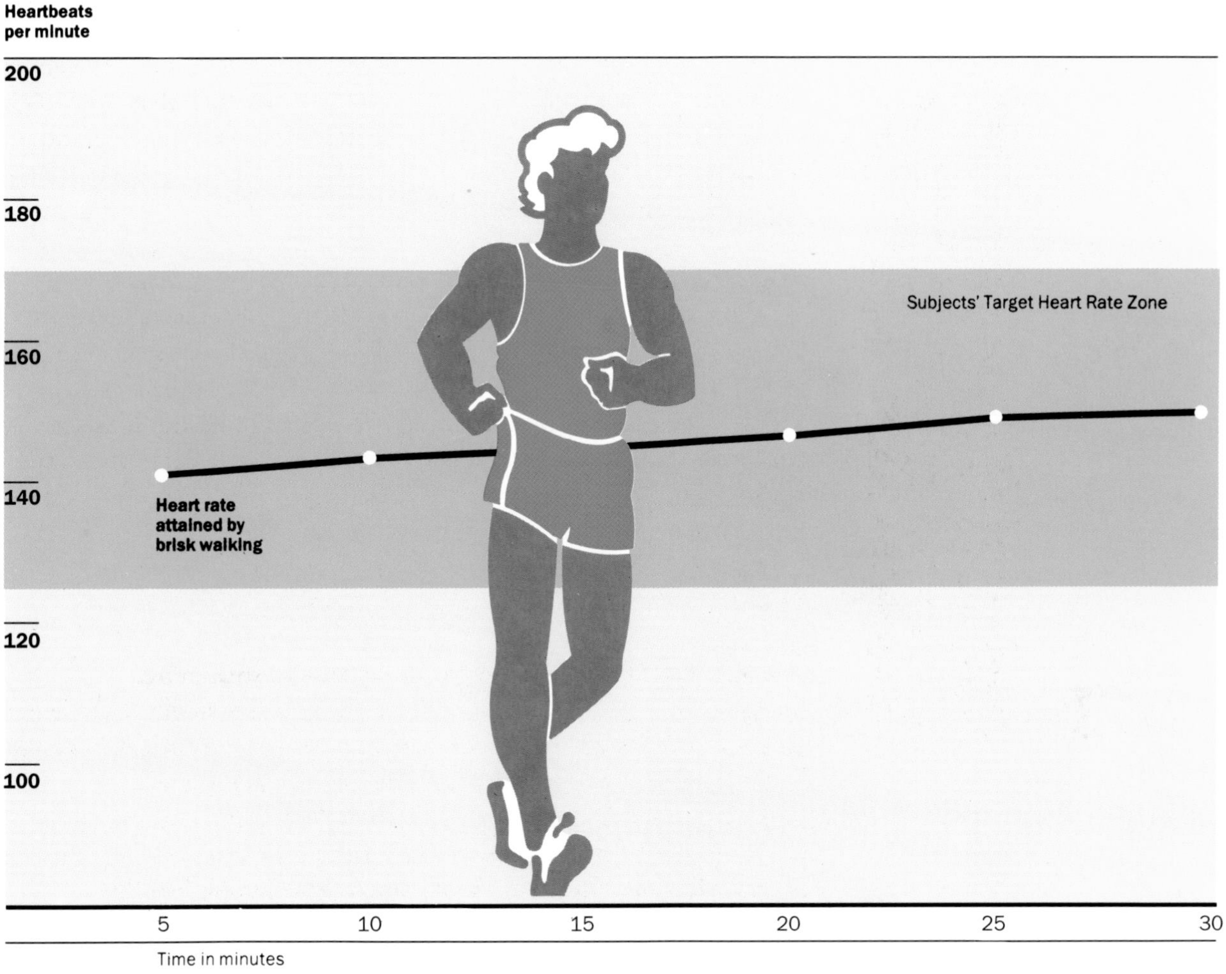

Even highly fit exercisers can benefit from walking. In one study, male subjects who ranged in age from 22 to 39 were told to walk for half an hour at a pace that would enable each of them to reach his target heart rate — a rate that varies with age and that indicates a person is exercising intensely enough to obtain aerobic benefits. As shown above, all the subjects achieved this level of intensity after the first five minutes and maintained it for the rest of the walk.

its healing qualities. Because of water's buoyancy, water exercises are non-weight-bearing, which means that they place no strain whatsoever on the injured body part. Also, physiologists believe that water increases circulation, which speeds the healing process. Then, too, water has a soothing effect that can relieve pain. Other types of soft workouts can also help during recuperation from an injury. Often, an exerciser will choose a routine that is a softened version of his or her usual workout — an injured runner may get back in shape via a walking programme, for example, or a high-impact aerobic dancer might shift to a low-impact movement routine.

How can you tell if you are working out at the correct intensity?
The classic way is to take your pulse, which will tell you whether you are reaching your target heart rate. (For the formula on how to

Boosting the Workout

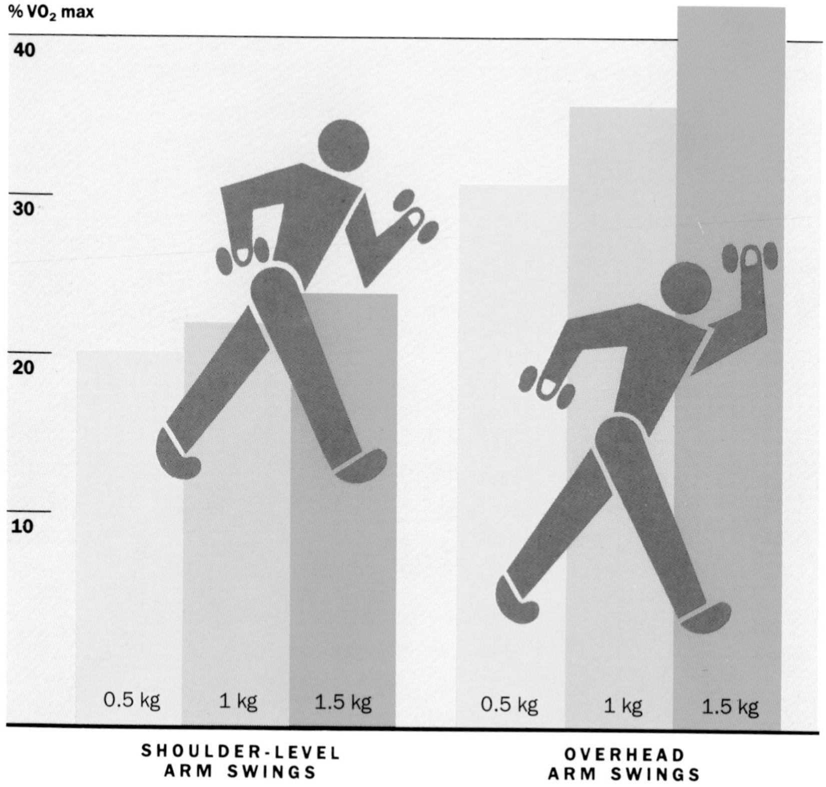

Swinging one's arms while carrying light hand weights can intensify a soft workout — and the more vigorous the arm swings, the better. One study examined the energy costs of walking workouts, as measured by VO_2 max, when various-sized weights were added. All the workouts showed increases in VO_2 max, but the change was most dramatic when the subjects walked while pumping their elbows up to ear level.

determine target heart rate, see page 21.) There are also two generally accepted rules of thumb. One is that if the workout makes you pant, you are working hard enough. The other rule is that you should still be able to hold a conversation comfortably while exercising; if you are breathing so hard that speaking is difficult or impossible, you are probably working yourself too hard.

Are there ways to boost the intensity of soft workouts?

Previously sedentary people who start a programme of walking or another low-impact workout may quickly find themselves much improved in fitness. For them, and for people who are already well trained yet want to soften their workouts for injury prevention, there are a number of ways to increase intensity to maintain continued effectiveness in improving fitness levels.

One method used in both walking and low-impact aerobic dance is to increase the work your arms are doing. One expert has calculated that keeping the arms in constant motion at shoulder level or above during exercise increases the heart rate enough to provide a moderate aerobic stimulus. In addition, many exercisers rely on portable weights to increase the energy costs of their workouts.

Hand weights have been shown to modestly increase oxygen consumption and heart rate as well as the number of calories burned during exercise — usually by 5 to 10 per cent. The most recent research suggests that the best approach to boosting your cardiovascular output is to combine controlled arm swinging and hand weights *(see illustration, opposite page)*. One study, for example, tested 20 men and women whose average age was 27, during normal walking, walking while vigorously swinging their arms, walking while carrying 1.5-kilogram hand weights and walking together with arm swinging while equipped with the weights. The researchers found that only the combination of weights and vigorous arm swinging had any significant impact on oxygen consumption and heart rate; weights alone were insufficient to do this. (Most authorities urge caution when adding hand weights to your routine, especially if you are in less than optimal condition, have a history of heart disease or suffer from chronic musculoskeletal problems, particularly lower back pain.)

Backpacks, too, may produce a workload sufficient to increase conditioning in trained individuals, although the research results have been mixed. One study of 44 men aged between 18 and 23 found that it was possible to improve the oxygen-uptake gains of a walking programme by carrying 3-kilogram backpacks. However, another study found that in order to reach their target heart rates, subjects had to carry an inordinate amount of baggage — the equivalent of some 40 per cent of their own body weight.

For quick, effective conditioning, try walking up and down stairs. Several workplace studies have found that people who began using stairs instead of lifts improved their fitness levels by 10 to 15 per cent. Stair climbing is a good calorie burner, too: you may use 17.5 calories per minute if you climb two steps per second.

What kind of soft workout should you do?

One of the appealing features of soft workouts is that they provide you with a number of accessible, low-injury exercise options. Research has shown that boredom is a key factor in fitness drop-out rates, so variety in an exercise programme is crucial. Many of the workouts that are illustrated here are interchangeable *(see chart, page 23)* and can be tailored to your personal exercise preferences. For example, you might prefer indoor, low-impact aerobic dance in the winter, but switch to walking outside during the warmer months. This workout flexibility will encourage you to exercise more regularly, an essential element in attaining and maintaining fitness. To see how soft workouts can benefit you, turn the page.

How to Design Your Own Programme

You can use soft workouts in a variety of ways: as your primary form of exercise, as an exercise substitute during recovery from an injury, or as a supplement to high-impact exercise. Additionally, you can alternate the different soft workouts themselves to provide your fitness programme with variety. This test, and the remaining pages in this chapter, will help you to determine how much exercise is appropriate for your level of fitness, as well as which soft workouts are the most suitable for your exercise needs.

Can you benefit from low-impact exercise?

1 Do you suffer occasional — or chronic — sports-related injuries?

Keeping injuries to a minimum is probably the most common reason for switching from a high-impact to a low-impact exercise programme. Indeed, it was the excessive rates of injury in many high-impact exercises that led to the development of low-impact alternatives. For example, water workouts are actually an offspring of hydrotherapy — rehabilitative exercise programmes in the water for injured or disabled persons. Because the risk of injury is greatly reduced in low-impact exercise, you are less likely to have to halt your workouts to allow for rest and recuperation. The more consistently you can exercise, the better able you will be to maintain your desired level of fitness. And even if you have to stop a high-impact exercise temporarily because of an injury, soft workouts can help maintain your conditioning so that you will have less difficulty getting up to speed when you are better.

2 Have you tried various forms of exercise, but repeatedly found yourself unable to stick to a programme?

Exercise drop-out rates are a common problem. Physical drawbacks such as injuries are only one of the difficulties; not having enough time or becoming bored after a few weeks or months can interfere with a workout programme. Achieving fitness does demand a commitment of time and consistency of effort: to gain cardiovascular benefits from aerobic exercise, you must work out in your target heart range for at least 20 minutes three times a week, plus five minutes each of warm-ups and cool-downs. Similarly, strength training and exercising to improve flexibility require workouts three or four times a week.

Soft workouts provide several different options to suit your personal preferences; you can alternate them for variety. Walking, in particular, can easily be fitted into any schedule and will allow you to achieve fitness benefits any time and anywhere. That is why more and more people — including many who have not exercised in years — are joining the ranks of walkers.

3 Are you overweight?

Soft workouts can benefit anyone, but one of their primary advantages is that they are appropriate for overweight individuals, pregnant women or others who for health reasons should not perform heavy weight-bearing exercises. If you are overweight or have a musculoskeletal problem such as weak knees or ankles, the pounding of high-impact exercise such as running and aerobic dance is even more damaging. Because soft workouts reduce or eliminate such impact, they can provide a safe exercise alternative for those for whom more stressful routines are inadvisable.

4 How far do you live from your workplace?

Walking is perhaps the ultimate low-impact exercise, in part because it can so easily be incorporated into the busiest schedule. And the fitness benefits of building exercise into your daily life might even protect against heart disease. A recent report issued by the Centers for Disease Control in the United States conclusively linked cardiac disease to a sedentary lifestyle; in fact, non-exercisers have almost twice as great a risk of coronary disease as their more fit counterparts. Researchers at the Centers suggest a regular schedule of moderate exercise such as walking. Another study suggests that those who seek optimum cardiovascular fitness to help to increase their longevity should expend 2,000 calories weekly in physical activity, the equivalent of walking briskly for about one hour a day, five times weekly.

To fit exercise into your existing schedule, try parking your car a few kilometres from work, or getting off the bus or train several stops before your accustomed destination and walking the remainder of the way. A brisk walk at lunchtime is another convenient, easy way of working out.

5 Are your swimming abilities below average?

The natural buoyancy of water makes swimming one of the best low-impact exercise options, but you need not be a swimmer to achieve the benefits of exercising in this ideal low-impact environment. Water workouts simply take land exercises — such as running, sit-ups, stretches for flexibility — and adjust them for a swimming pool. Research has shown that these exercises have the same metabolic benefits in the water as on land. Indeed, the resistance of the water, which is almost 800 times heavier than air, can increase the effectiveness of some exercises without increasing the stress on your musculoskeletal system.

6 Is a low-impact fitness programme sufficient if you are already fit?

Low-impact exercise is not low-intensity exercise. Studies have shown that most people are able to achieve their target heart rates with fast walking. And low-impact aerobic dance is in some ways more difficult than high-impact as it requires greater co-ordination. (The movement routines on pages 102-123 will help increase your co-ordination and flexibility, and improve your ability to perform other types of exercise effectively.) However, if you are very fit you might need to increase the effort of a soft workout by adding light hand weights while walking, dancing or working out in the water. Not only will this increase your heart rate, it will provide extra strengthening benefits.

Rating Your Fitness Level

To determine how fit you are currently and to monitor your progress during your exercise programme, you can take the Rockport Fitness Walking Test on the right. This test, which was developed for the Rockport Walking Institute in the United States by cardiologists and exercise scientists, is quite safe and can be taken by anyone. However, if you are over 35 years old, or if you have had any signs of heart disease, you should consult a doctor before performing it. The test will give you a simple but accurate measurement of your cardiovascular endurance. The only equipment you need is a stopwatch to clock both your pulse and your walking time over one mile — 1.6 kilometres.

After taking the test, see how your results relate to the graph for your age and sex, on the far right. You will fall into one of five fitness categories. If the results show that you are at a low or below average level of fitness, the workouts in this book will help you improve your fitness level significantly.

As your fitness builds, or if you have already reached an average, above average or high level of fitness, you can increase the exertion of soft workouts by adding weights or following the other guidelines for intensifying exercise that are given in the following chapters. Take the test periodically — every month or two — to keep track of how your endurance is improving.

The Rockport Fitness Walking Test

Step 1 Record your resting heart rate. Walk on the spot for 30 seconds, then use the tips of your second and third fingers to find the radial artery in your wrist. First feel for the wristbone at the base of the thumb, then move your fingertips down your wrist until you find your pulse. Count your pulse for 15 seconds and multiply it by four to determine the rate per minute.

Step 2 Find a measured track or measure out a level 1.6 kilometres. Then walk 1.6 kilometres as fast as you can. Record your time precisely at the end of the distance. (Walking speeds may vary in individuals, so you may want to repeat this test at a later date to make sure your first 1.6 kilometre time is typical for you.)

Step 3 Immediately record your heart rate at the end of the 1.6 kilometres.

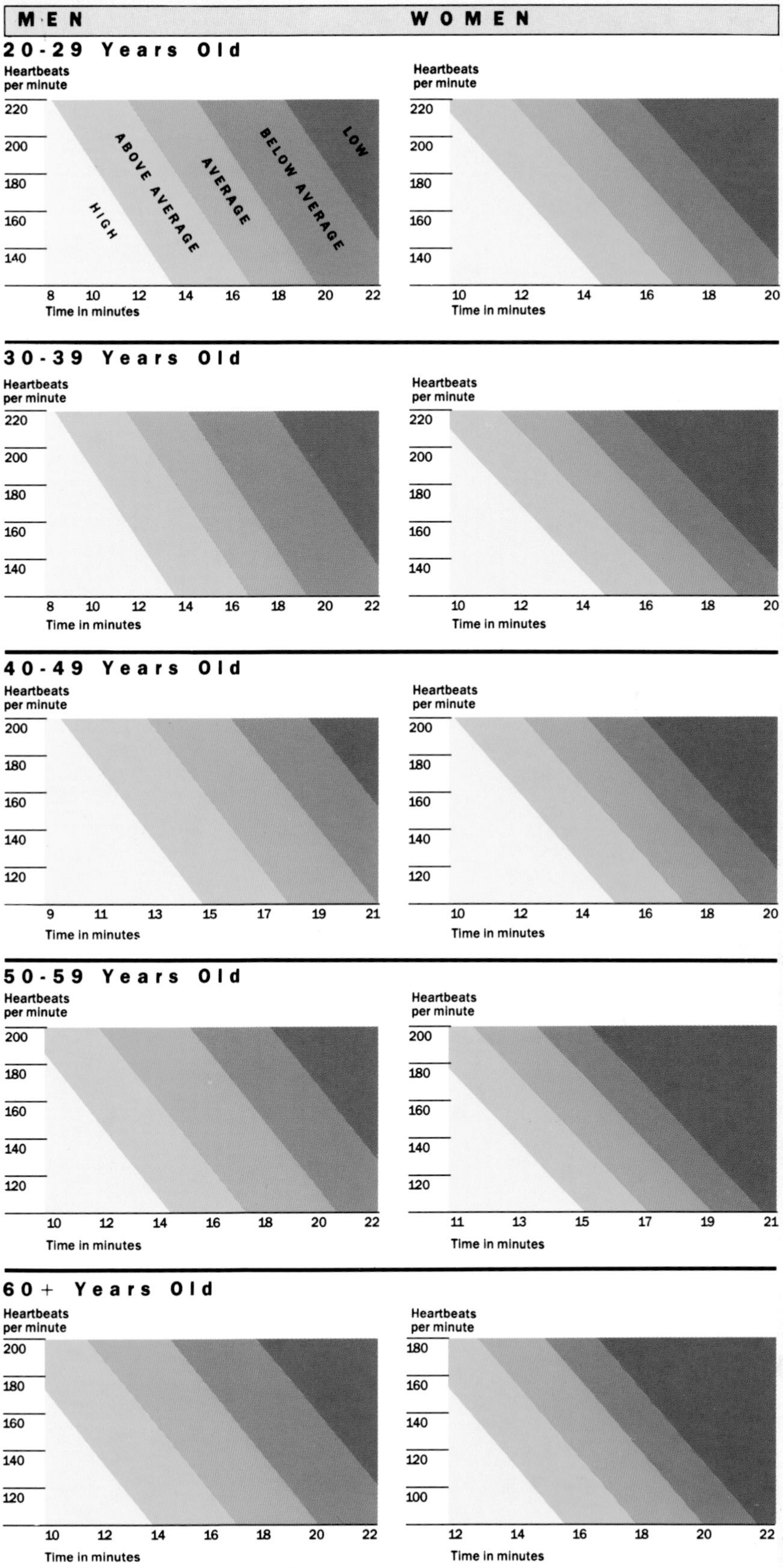

Choosing an Exercise

Soft workouts can encompass the four essential components of a fitness programme, as the diagrams opposite indicate. This volume provides endurance conditioning by means of low-impact aerobic exercises; muscle strengtheners that rely on light weights or that are performed against the resistance of water; non-ballistic flexibility exercises; and movement routines that make use of the body's resistance to gravity to enhance co-ordination.

Some of the exercises on the following pages target more than one area of fitness. For example, walking with weights not only boosts your cardiovascular system, it also strengthens your arm muscles. However, no single exercise provides benefits in all four categories. To get a comprehensive workout, you should perform exercises targeted at different fitness goals.

The soft workouts in the following three chapters provide several exercise options for each category of fitness. You may combine these components in various ways. For example, you might decide on a complete fitness programme in the water. Or you may prefer water workouts to promote strength and flexibility, a walking programme for endurance and movement routines for improved co-ordination. Varying your set of exercises will keep your workouts interesting and challenging.

Targeting Your Workout

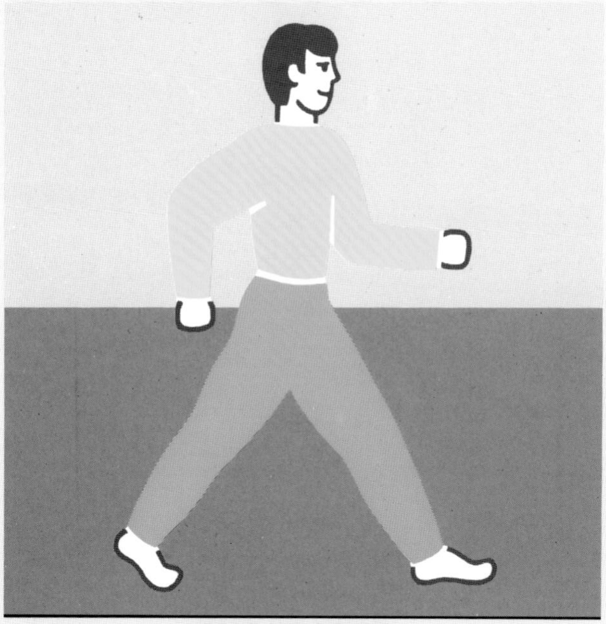

ENDURANCE

Aerobic exercise, which requires sustained activity that engages the large muscle groups of the body, stimulates the body's cardiovascular system and builds endurance.

low-impact dance *pages 36-53* **walking** *pages 64-69*
water workouts *pages 86-89*

STRENGTH

Muscles grow stronger as greater demands are placed on them, either by increasing repetitions of a particular muscular action or by adding resistance — usually weights — to intensify the activity.

low-impact dance *pages 56-61* **walking** *pages 66-67*
water workouts *pages 76-81*

FLEXIBILITY

Flexibility is achieved through stretching exercises that develop the full range of motion in the muscles and joints. Stretching enhances your ability to perform exercises without injury and is an important component of warm-up routines.

water workouts *pages 82-85, 96-97* **movement** *pages 102-103*

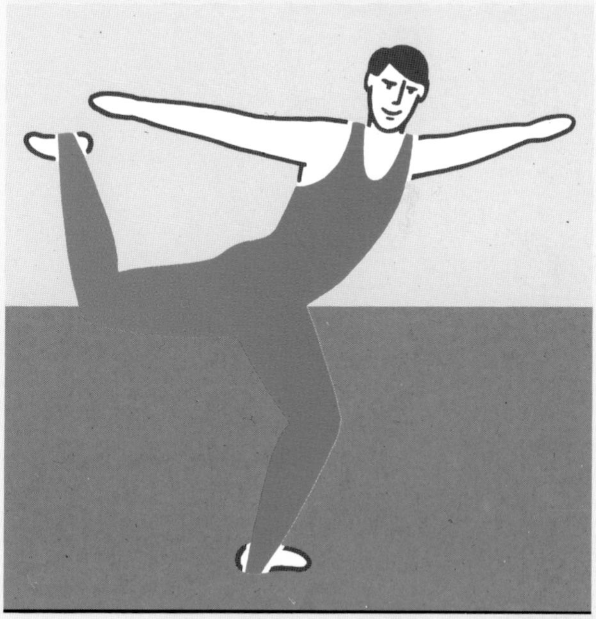

CO-ORDINATION

Good co-ordination improves agility and is essential for the successful execution of any sport and most exercises. Moving your body in predetermined sequences that require concentration and body awareness helps develop this important aspect of fitness.

water workouts *pages 90-95* **movement** *pages 102-123*

NIKE

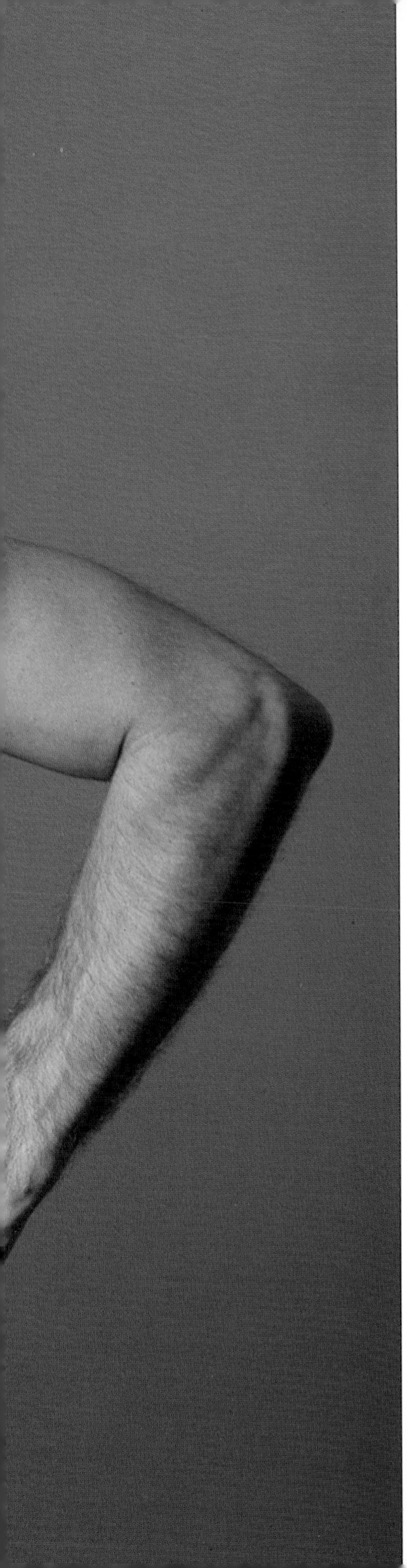

CHAPTER TWO

Aerobics

The key: combining arms and legs

Aerobic exercise, which uses repeated continuous, rhythmic movements of the large muscle groups — primarily the arms and legs — to boost the cardiovascular system, forms the cornerstone of any basic fitness programme. Low-impact aerobic exercise, which includes both walking and aerobic dance, also encompasses such standard cardiovascular strengtheners as cycling, rowing and swimming.

When participants in low-impact dance and fitness walking programmes exercise vigorously, they can reach and maintain their target heart rates for at least 20 minutes — the amount of time it takes to receive cardiovascular benefits from exercise, as determined by the American College of Sports Medicine. (To determine your target heart rate zone, subtract your age from 220. Multiply the remainder by 0.65 to determine the low end of the range and by 0.85 to calculate the high end. For cardiovascular conditioning, your pulse should fall between these two figures during aerobic exercise.) One study of middle-aged men found that those who walked for 40 minutes a day, four days a week for 20 weeks showed cardiovascular improvements equal to participants in a 30-minute-a-day, three-times-a-week running programme. A study of participants in aerobic dance classes indicated that they, too, achieved cardiovascular conditioning through regular workouts, with significant improvements after only six weeks.

The distinguishing feature of low-impact aerobic dance is that one foot always remains in contact with the floor. The jumping and bouncing inherent in high-impact aerobic dance — and at the root of most dance-related injuries — are replaced by walking, marching, side-stepping and lunging. An increase in upper-body work compensates for the reduced demands on the lower body. Because performing arm movements at or above the level of the heart helps boost your heart rate, vigorous but controlled arm work is essential.

Jumping in high-impact aerobics practically ensures that you will boost your heart rate. In contrast, the aerobic benefits of low-impact routines come from carefully choreographed combinations of arm and leg work. These routines must be performed with precision in order to achieve any cardiovascular benefits, so low-impact routines require greater concentration and co-ordination than do high-impact ones.

To allow for the more deliberate co-ordination of low-impact dance, the music you use to pace yourself should be slightly slower — between 125 and 145 beats per minute — than it is for high-impact routines. If you are incorporating weights into your routine, choose music with a tempo of 120 to 140 beats per minute. Counting to the beat of the music will keep you working at the proper intensity as well as help you co-ordinate your movements.

Most injuries sustained in an aerobic dance programme occur below the knee — shin splints, Achilles tendinitis and stress fractures. Reducing the impact lessens the stress on the lower body, but the increased lateral floor movements and arm use in low-impact routines can result in injuries to the back, shoulders, arms or knees. Taking a few precautions during your workout will minimize the risks. Maintain proper posture: abdominal muscles contracted, buttocks tucked under and knees slightly bent. When lunging, make sure that your bent knees never extend beyond your toes to avoid excess stress on ankle and knee ligaments; your knee should also always be pointed in the same direction as your lower leg. Be careful not to arch your back when working the upper body: keeping your pelvis tilted forwards and your knees relaxed will avoid this. Arm movements should be smooth and controlled; jerky arm movements can hyperextend and possibly injure the shoulder and elbow joints, forearms and wrists.

Like low-impact dance, walking is a grounded activity — one foot lands before the other pushes off. The foot rolls forwards from heel landing to forefoot push-off, which spreads the propulsive and impact forces across a larger surface of the foot than running does *(see illustration, page 10)*. Day-to-day walking is usually performed at a rate of

Caring for Your Feet

Your feet, which contain 26 bones and more than 20 muscles, endure much of the stress of weight-bearing exercise — including walking and low-impact aerobic dance. Foot injuries associated with exercise range from simple blisters to painful heel spurs. Many such problems can be eliminated or reduced through proper foot care. The following suggestions will help you maintain the health of your feet and, in turn, exercise in greater comfort.

- **Wear well-fitting shoes suited to your particular activity. Shoes that fit will feel comfortable as soon as you put them on; if you think they will need a breaking-in period, do not buy them. (For specific information on walking and aerobic shoes, turn the page.)**

- **Wash your feet daily with soap and warm water. Dry well, especially between the toes, an area prone to athlete's foot. Apply a non-lanolin moisturizing cream to dry skin on your heels or toes.**

- **Use foot powder. Apply an antifungal foot powder after cleaning your feet and also sprinkle it in your shoes to help absorb perspiration.**

- **Protect blister-prone areas on your feet with petroleum jelly before you exercise. If you do develop a large, painful blister, you can relieve the pressure by draining it: cleanse it with an antiseptic solution and puncture round the edge with a sterile needle. Apply a topical antibiotic and cover. Keep your foot dry for a day or two to avoid infection.**

- **Do not treat other foot ailments yourself. Contact your doctor or chiropodist if you notice any persistent abrasion, rash or abnormality. Never try to cut away your own corns or bunions.**

3 to 5 kilometres per hour. Depending on your level of conditioning, you need to walk between 5.5 and 7 kilometres per hour for optimum fitness. You must use your arms as you do in low-impact aerobic dance. Vigorous arm swinging will increase the effort demanded of walking, making it a fitness exercise.

As your aerobic fitness increases from either a walking or low-impact dance regimen, you will find that it becomes increasingly difficult to reach your target heart rate. This shows that your heart muscle has adapted to the workload and become more efficient. Increasing movements that cross the floor and doing more arm work at shoulder level or higher will increase cardiovascular demands. You can further intensify your workouts by incorporating light hand-held or wrist weights. Adding weights, when combined with arm swinging, has been shown to increase oxygen consumption, heart rate and calories burned during exercise. Excluding warm-ups and cool-downs, you can use weights with any of the aerobic dance routines on the following pages. Exercises designed to strengthen particular muscles are shown on pages 56-61. Intensifying your walking programme with weights is shown on pages 66-67. Retro, or backwards, walking, demonstrated on pages 68-69, is a way to add variety to your walking programme.

The Right Footwear

The only essential equipment for both walking and low-impact aerobic dance is an appropriate pair of shoes. Shoes for low-impact aerobic dance should feature good forefoot stability to accommodate the sideways movement that largely replaces the jumping of high-impact aerobic dance. Look for a reinforced band round the arch of the shoe and a firm heel counter, which wraps round the heel to help stabilize the foot. The shoes should also have a flexed or notched outer sole for traction and flexibility.

Some shoes with these features are designed specifically for low-impact activity, such as the shoe on the bottom left. However, most standard aerobic-dance shoes are also acceptable for low-impact aerobics, although a high-top aerobic shoe, such as the one pictured on the top left, will provide extra lateral support.

Running and walking shoes are not interchangeable. The thick, shock-absorbing soles of running shoes make for unstable walking, so walking shoes feature less cushioning. They also have a rounded crash pad to absorb heelstrike. A walking shoe is more flexible than a running shoe so that the walking shoe can bend at a 45-degree angle at push-off; running shoes need flex to only 30 degrees. More grooves cut across the bottom of the walking shoe in conjunction with lower heel cushioning contribute to greater flexibility.

Walking shoes are styled to fit different needs. There are smart walking shoes, top right; rugged walking shoes for hiking or rough terrain, bottom right; and fitness walking shoes for workouts, bottom centre.

Wear socks when exercising to protect both your feet and your shoes from perspiration.

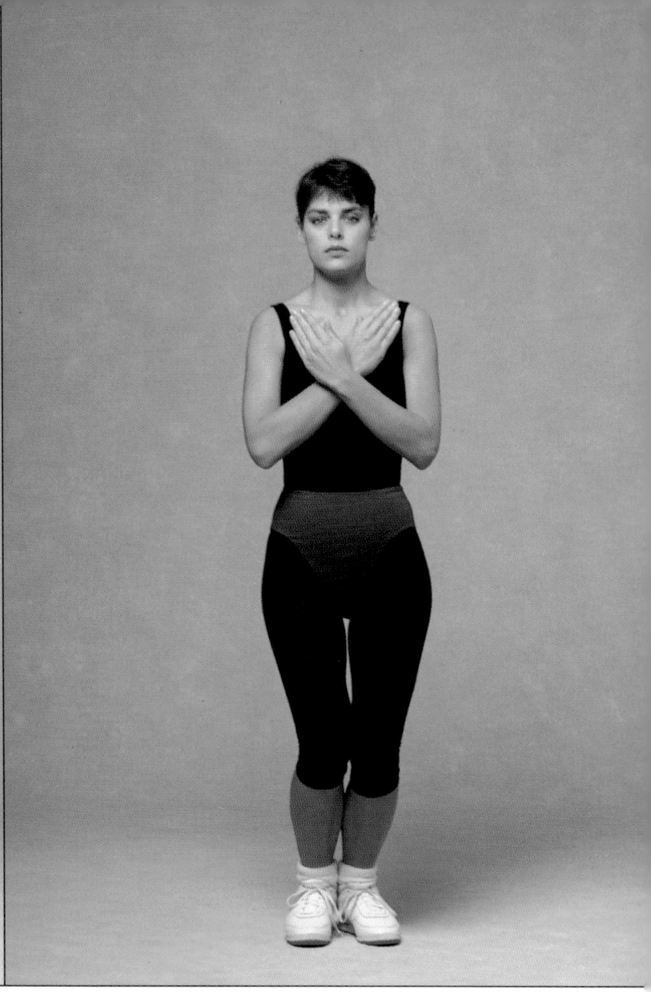

Setting Your Routine

The routine that follows progresses from elementary sequences that focus on arm work to more complicated steps requiring you to move across the floor. Begin the routine with the warm-ups on this page and the following five pages; they should be sustained for at least five minutes. The cool-downs on pages 54-55 should also be done for a minimum of five minutes.

Following the warm-ups is a series of exercises in which you lunge, march, roll up on your toes and use your arms, but essentially stay in one place. These precede the more complicated moving-around steps, in which you move across the floor. Combination sequences couple the arm work of stationary sequences with the movement steps. Each sequence should be performed symmetrically: if you first move to your left, you should then reverse directions and repeat the exercise to your right. Do each sequence four times.

You will probably get the most benefit — and enjoyment, too — from your low-impact routine if you mix the steps in different combinations and move in different directions. You can combine sequences that use side-to-side movement with those that go forwards and backwards, interspersed with moving-on-the-spot steps. Be sure to vary the height of your arm movements.

As you get stronger, you will find that it becomes more difficult to achieve your target heart rate. To make your dancing more demanding, do more knee bends, take longer steps and concentrate more on moving-around sequences. You can further intensify your workout by adding hand or wrist weights. Strengthening exercises that involve using weights are demonstrated on pages 56-61. For maximum benefit, you should perform the routines four to five times a week.

Warm-Ups/1

Stand up straight with your arms lifted slightly to the side and your right leg extended; point your toes *(far left)*. Bend your knees as you bring your feet together and swing your arms so that they cross in front of your chest *(centre)*. Straighten your right leg as you repeat to your left side *(left)*.

After warming up, you can increase the intensity of the above routine by raising your arms on the extension phase. Start by bringing them to shoulder height *(left)*. When you can do this comfortably, raise them over your head *(below)*.

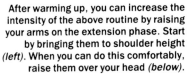

Warm-Ups/2

Stand with your feet shoulder-width apart, toes pointed outwards and arms at your sides with your palms facing downwards. Bend your knees and push off on your left foot, leaning to the right and lifting your left shoulder *(left)*. Bend your knees again to recentre your weight *(centre)*. Push off to your left, lifting your right shoulder and pointing your right foot.

Warm-Ups/3

Stand with your feet together and knees bent. Bring your elbows back to chest height, with your palms facing forwards *(right)*. Simultaneously push your hands forwards and thrust your right foot out, resting it on its heel *(below)*. Return to the starting position and switch legs.

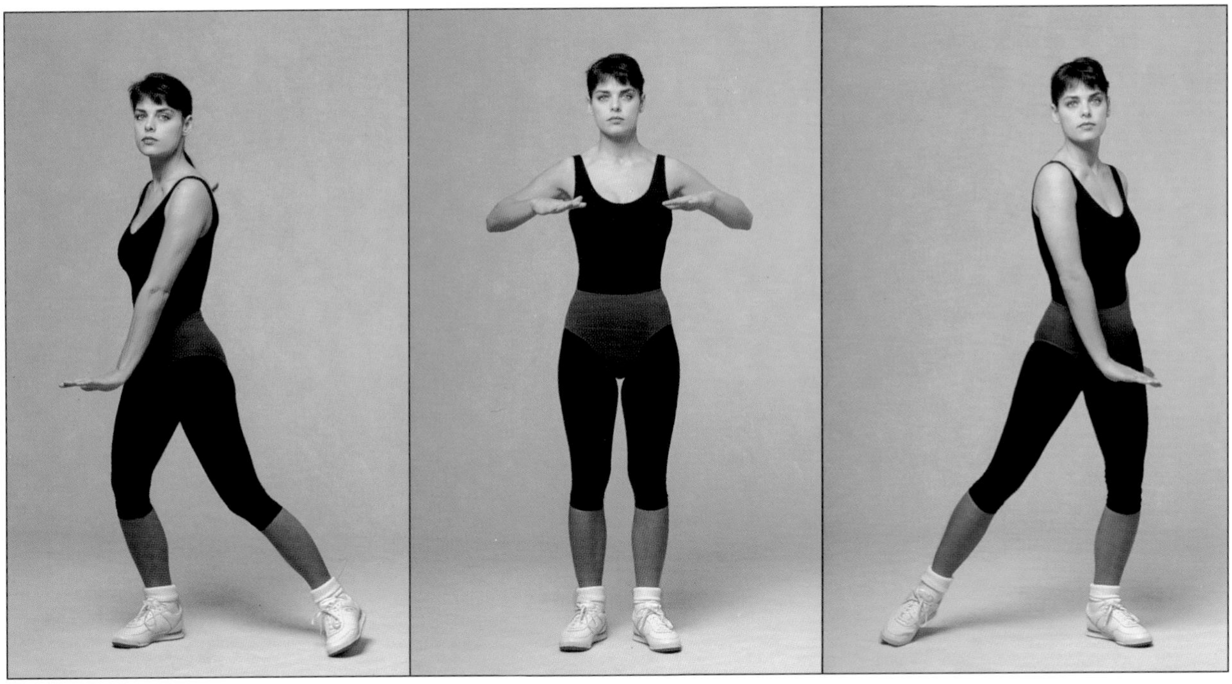

From a standing position with your arms at your sides, rotate your torso and swivel your right foot to the right as you bend your right knee. Push your hands down on either side of your body *(left)*. Bring your left foot in to your right, at the same time raising your arms in front of your chest *(centre)*. Rotate to your left *(above)* and return to the centre. When bending your knees, do not extend them further than your toes.

Moving on the Spot/1

Stand straight with your shoulders relaxed, your abdomen contracted and your buttocks tucked under. Vigorously march on the spot, bringing each knee high and keeping your foot positioned directly beneath it. Land on the ball of your foot and rock to the heel on impact. Pump with your arms, holding your elbows flexed at 90-degree angles. Continue for a minute or more. You can use this as a transition step between routines.

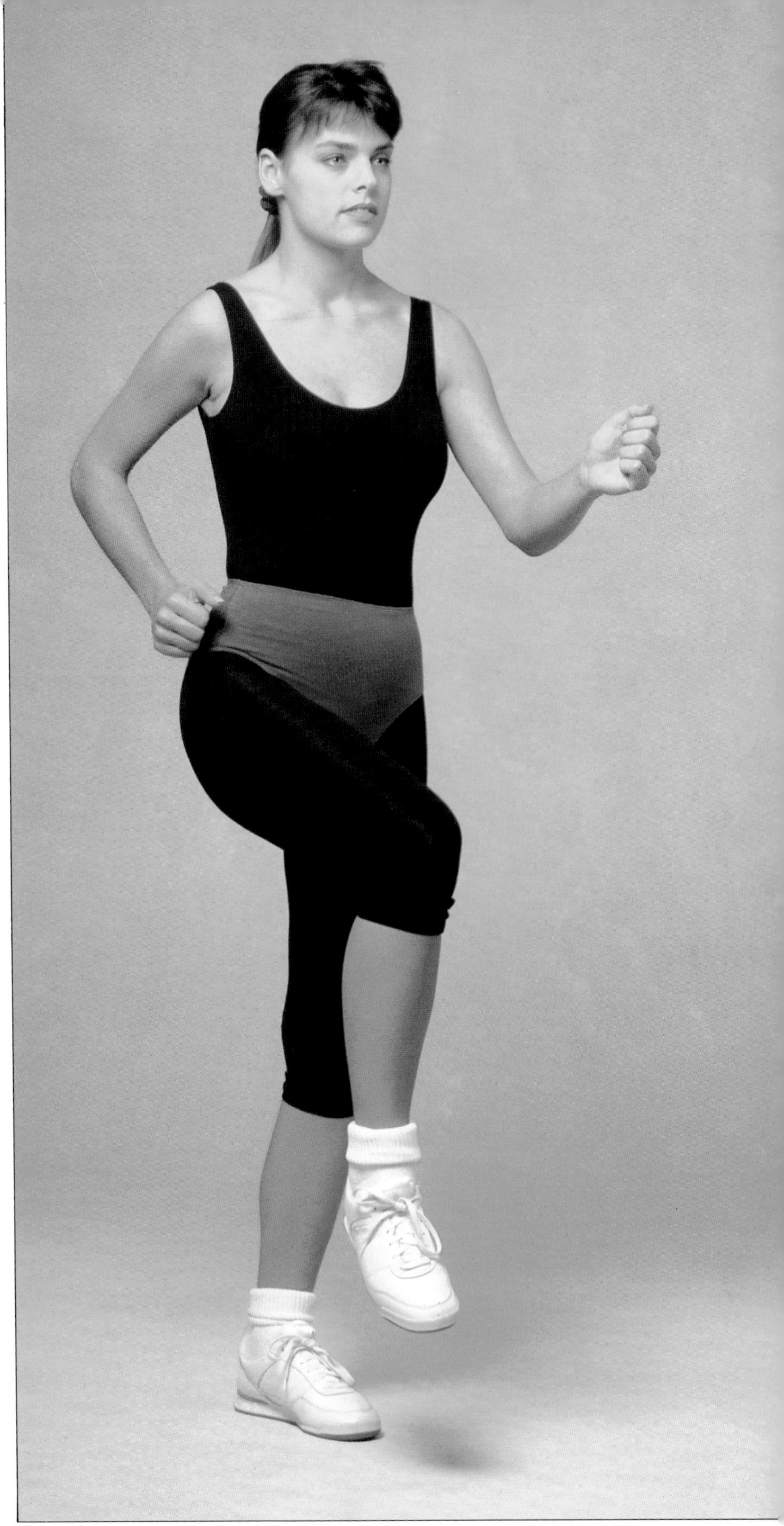

Stand with your feet together and your arms extended in front of you at shoulder height, your palms facing downwards *(left)*. Tilt your pelvis forwards and point the toes of your right foot as you make your hands into fists and forcefully pull your arms in to your sides *(below)*. Repeat with your left leg.

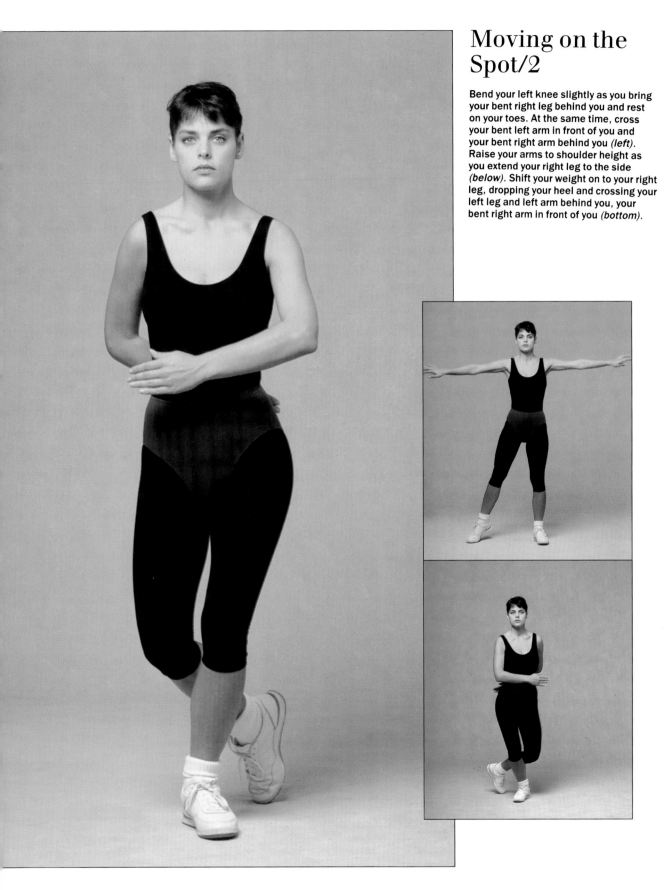

Moving on the Spot/2

Bend your left knee slightly as you bring your bent right leg behind you and rest on your toes. At the same time, cross your bent left arm in front of you and your bent right arm behind you *(left)*. Raise your arms to shoulder height as you extend your right leg to the side *(below)*. Shift your weight on to your right leg, dropping your heel and crossing your left leg and left arm behind you, your bent right arm in front of you *(bottom)*.

Bend your arms and hold them at shoulder height. Roll them over each other and rotate your torso slightly to the left as you extend your right leg to the side, pointing your toes *(above)*. Bend your knees as you bring your right leg back to your left *(right)*.

Moving on the Spot/3

Bend your right arm upwards and touch your right elbow with your left hand. Lift your right hip as you move your right leg to the side *(below)*. Shift your weight on to your right foot and bring your left foot into your right *(centre)*. Transfer your weight on to your left foot *(right)*, then back to your right.

Bend your arms so that your hands are behind your shoulders and point your right foot in front of you *(top)*. Take a small step forwards on to your right foot as you swing your arms forwards *(centre)*. Point your left foot behind you, then swing your arms up as you step back on to your left foot and point the toes of your right foot *(right)*. Leading with your right foot, march on the spot for seven steps; then repeat the entire sequence, beginning with your left foot.

Moving on the Spot/4

Stand up straight with your feet together. Simultaneously step to the right on to the ball of your right foot and raise your right arm over your head *(left)*. Then step to the left on to the ball of your left foot as you raise your left arm over your head *(centre, left)*. Bend your left knee as you step in with your right foot and bend your right elbow, pulling your arm in to your chest *(centre, right)*. Bend both knees, bringing your left foot in to your right and pulling your left arm in to your chest *(above)*.

Moving Around/1

Bend your arms at the elbow, keeping your fingers straight. Step forwards on to your right foot *(below)*. Rotate your arms at the elbow in a locomotive-like motion as you step forwards on to your left foot *(centre, left)*, then forwards on to your right *(centre, right)*. Touch your left foot to your right instep *(right)*. Step backwards on to your left foot. Continue backwards with two more steps, then touch your right foot to your left instep.

Repeat the walking sequence shown on the left but bring your arms to shoulder height, using an alternate punching motion with each step.

Moving Around/2

Clockwise from top left: raise your arms to shoulder height and extend your right leg, pointing your toes. Shift your weight on to your right foot as you bend your left knee and bring your left foot behind your right, bending your elbows in to your waist. Shift your weight back to your left foot and again extend your right leg to the side with your arms outstretched. Bring your elbows back in to your waist as you shift on to your right foot and bring your left foot in next to your right instep.

Increase the arm work in the preceding sequence by clapping your hands over your head for the final step *(right)*. You can also cross your arms in front of you on the arm extensions, alternating the arm that is on top *(below)*.

Combinations/1

Bend your elbows and bring your arms to shoulder height. Leading with your left foot, take three steps forwards, punching in front of you with alternate arms *(left)*. On the fourth step, bring your right foot forwards as far as your left instep *(centre, left)*. Step back with your right foot as you bring your right arm back to your chest *(centre, right)*. Kick your left foot forwards and push out with your arms *(right)*. Bring your arms back in to your chest and step backwards with your left foot. Kick your right foot forwards, extending your arms. Go back two more steps, kick, then lower your right foot next to your left.

Combinations/2

Lift your arms up over your head and, turning to your left, bring your right leg up to hip height *(far left)*. Bend your elbows and drop your arms and leg; repeat, then pivot to your right and lift your arms upwards again, this time lifting your left knee *(centre, left)*. Drop your leg and arms, repeat, then pivot back to your left, kicking your right foot forwards and pushing back with your arms *(centre, right)*. Bring your arms and leg back to the centre, then repeat once more. Pivot to your right and kick with your left leg twice *(above)*.

Combinations/3

Swing your arms and hips to the right as you lean in to your right hip *(below)*, then swing to the left; repeat. On the final swing, bring your left foot behind your right *(centre)*. Rise on to the toes of your left foot and step to the right with your right leg, swinging your arms back to the right. Touch the ball of your left foot to your right instep, then extend your leg out to the left as you clap your hands overhead *(right)*.

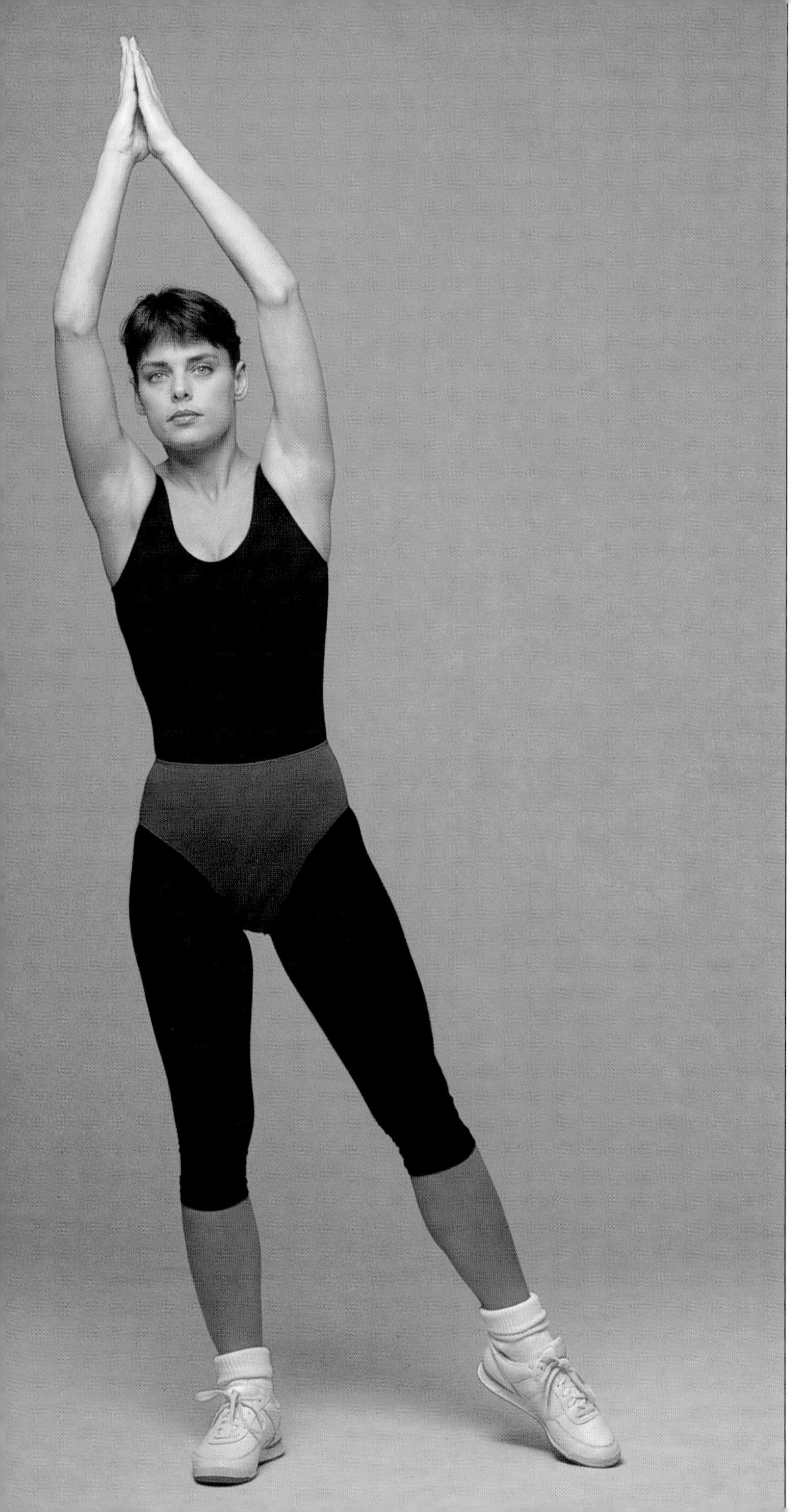

Cool-Downs

Stand with your feet about shoulder-width apart, your toes pointing outwards. Bend your knees slightly as you rotate your right arm at the shoulder, bringing it downwards in a crawl-like swimming motion *(left)*. Straighten your legs and bring your right shoulder back, then flex your knees again as you repeat with your left arm *(below)*.

From a standing position, raise your arms in front of you to shoulder level and bend your knees *(above)*. Start to swing your arms down and straighten your knees. Bring your arms behind you, bending your knees again *(centre)*, then swing your arms up towards the ceiling. Straighten your body as you extend your arms overhead *(right)*.

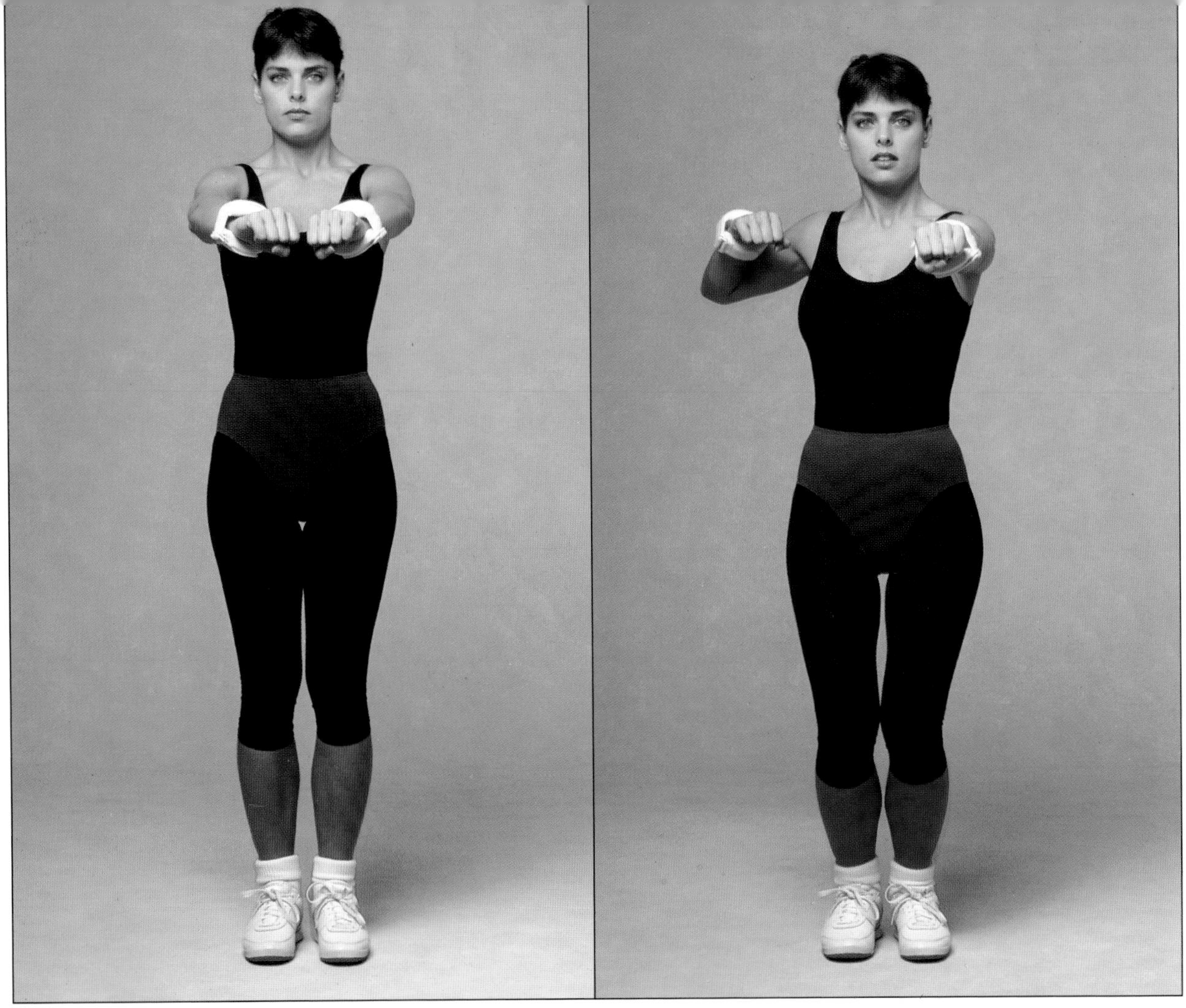

Stand with your knees bent slightly and your arms raised to shoulder level *(above, left)*. Bend your knees, pulling your bent right arm backwards so your fist is about level with your shoulder *(above)*. Straighten your legs as you return to the starting position, then repeat with your left arm.

Adding Weights/1

Weights help to intensify an aerobic dance programme, but they should only be incorporated once you can easily perform your usual routine without reaching your target heart rate. An indication of the right time to add weights is when you can perform 16 repetitions of the same step without becoming fatigued. This is a sign that your body has adapted to a higher level of fitness. By using additional weights you will place more demands on your cardiovascular system, boosting your heart rate back into its target range.

Begin by using the lightest hand weights that are available. (Because of the stress that they add to the shin, the Achilles tendon and the back, ankle weights are not recommended for use during aerobic exercise.) As your body adapts to this new load, you will be able to increase the weights gradually. Do not attempt to use weights that are heavier than 1.5 kilograms each when performing low-impact aerobics.

Hold the weights firmly but not tightly — the isometric pressure of tight gripping can impair your blood flow in the arms and thus raise blood pressure. If you develop muscle pain or joint soreness, stop using weights until the pain disappears. Visit your doctor immediately if the pain persists. When you are ready to take up weights again, start off with a light load, and increase it gradually.

Stand with your knees slightly bent and your arms at your sides with your elbows bent *(right)*. Move both arms behind you as far as possible, keeping your elbows bent *(below)*. Return to the starting position.

Stand with your legs shoulder-width apart and your arms outstretched at shoulder height. Lunge to the left as you extend your left arm and bend your right elbow *(above)*.

Adding Weights/2

From a standing position with your arms at your sides, step to your right, so your feet are shoulder-width apart and your knees are bent. Your arms should be at shoulder height with your elbows flexed *(below)*. Simultaneously pull your elbows in to your sides and bring your right foot back to the centre *(centre)*. Repeat the arm motion as you step to your left. Vary the motion by raising your arms over your head when you step in *(right)*, then pulling them down to shoulder height when you step out. Keep your elbows bent when you raise your arms over your head.

Adding Weights/3

Raise your bent arms to shoulder height. As you lift your left knee to hip level *(right)*, pull your arms down to touch slightly under your bent knee *(below)*, then bring the arms back up as you put your left leg down and raise your right. Keep your back straight.

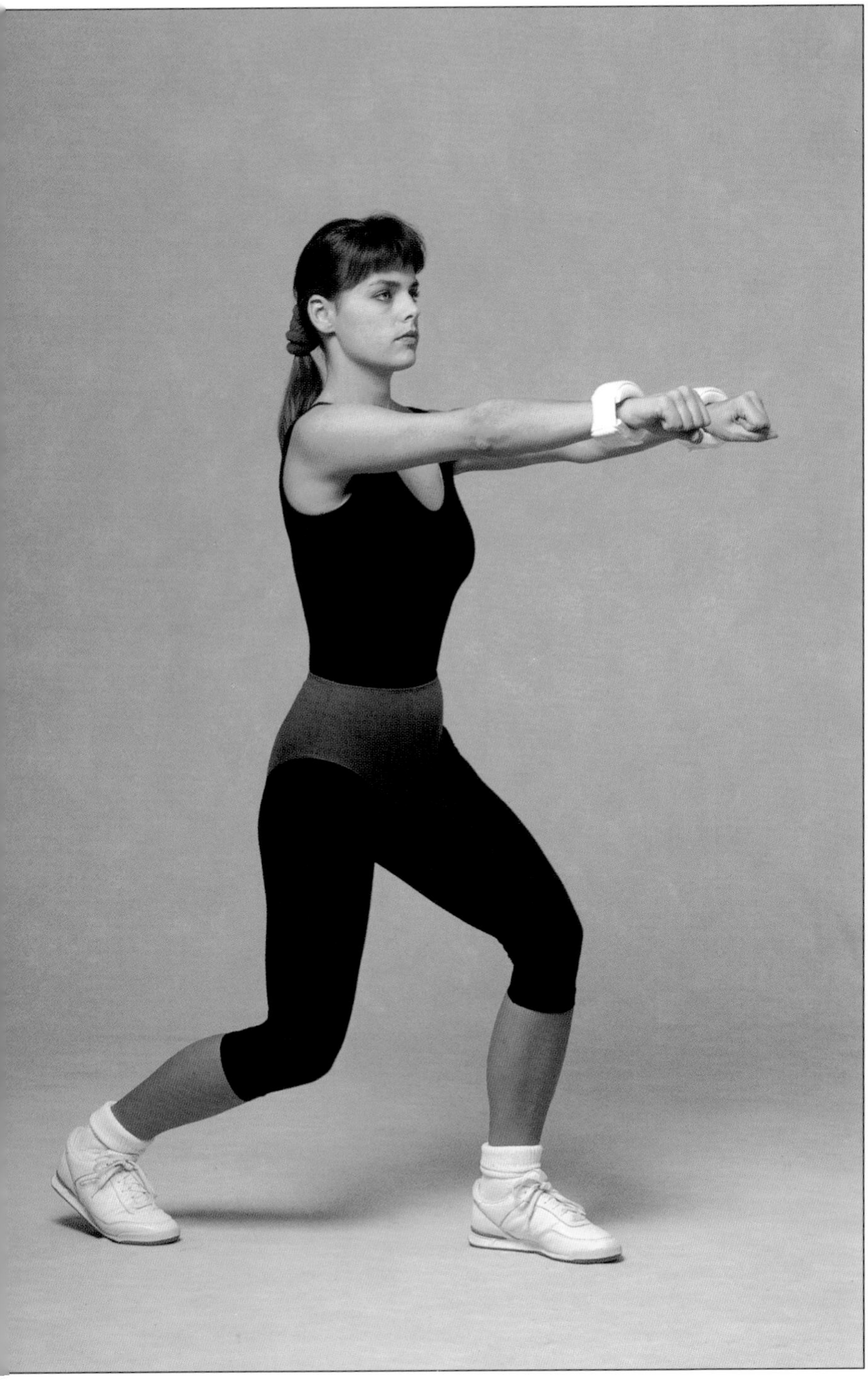

From a standing position, extend your arms directly in front of you. Push off on your left foot to lunge backwards on to the ball of your right foot. Keep your back knee bent *(left)*. Return to the starting position by pushing off your back foot and bringing your arms in to your chest.

Your Walking Programme

When performed aerobically, walking provides important cardiovascular benefits comparable to those that are associated with more strenuous types of aerobic exercise such as running and cycling. Numerous studies have confirmed that walking can improve circulation and lung capacity.

To achieve aerobic benefits from walking or any other activity, you need to exercise vigorously enough to attain your target heart rate, then sustain it for at least 20 minutes. Researchers have found that most individuals are able to reach their target heart rates at walking speeds of between 5.5 and 7 kilometres an hour. Changing your pace from strolling (at 5 kilometres an hour or slower) to striding (at 6.5 kilometres an hour or faster) increases your energy expenditure, as measured in calories, by up to a third, as the chart opposite shows. To determine your walking pace, see the chart at the bottom of the opposite page.

When you walk at a moderate pace, your level of exertion approaches that of swimming, as the chart below shows. If you intensify your walking workout, as demonstrated on pages 66-67, your energy output will approximate to that of slow running; however, your body will not be at risk from the physical stresses that contribute to the high rate of running injuries. The biomechanical aspects of walking are explained on pages 64-65. Retro walking, which is a way of working your muscles differently and adding variety to your walking regimen, is described on pages 68-69.

WALKING VS. OTHER ACTIVITIES

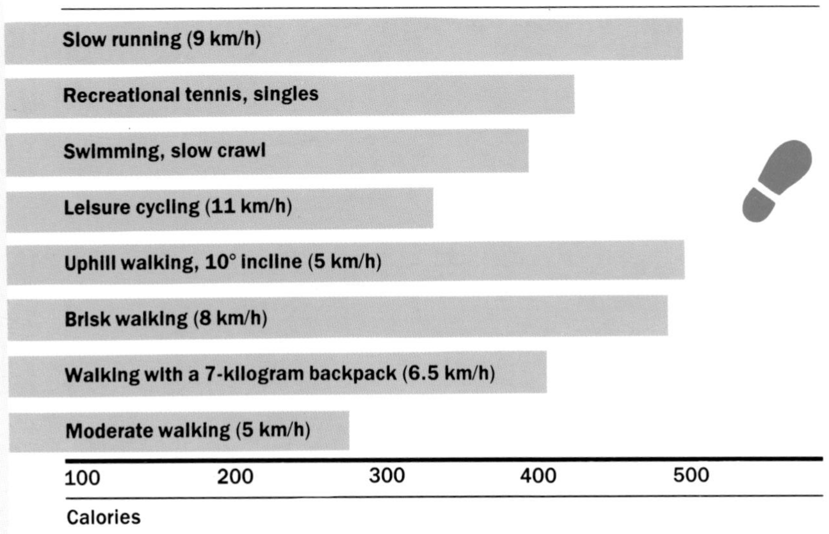

This chart compares the number of calories expended by a 68-kilogram person during one hour of various activities. Add 10 per cent for every 7 kilograms over this weight; subtract 10 per cent for every 7 kilograms under.

CALORIES BURNED BY WALKING FOR ONE HOUR

	WEIGHT IN KILOGRAMS					
km/h	45	55	65	70	80	90
5	180	220	260	300	340	380
5.5	220	260	300	340	380	420
6.5	250	300	350	400	450	500
7	280	340	400	460	520	580
8	320	380	450	530	610	690

WALKING SPEED CONVERSION TABLE

Steps per minute	Minutes per km	Km per hour
70	20	3
90	15	4
105	12	5
120	10	6
140	9	6.5
160	8	7.5
175	7	8.5
190	6.5	9
210+	<6	>10

To estimate your walking speed, count how many steps you take per minute and compare the results with this table. This rate is based on an average stride (0.75 metres long); stride length will vary from person to person.

Biomechanics of Walking

For fitness walking, your forward arm should be bent at about a 90-degree angle, with your fists clenched loosely *(top)*. The arm behind you should just brush your side as it pumps forwards and the other arm swings backwards *(above)*.

Walking conditions the whole body, but particularly the legs. The flexing of your foot when it lands strengthens the shins, while pushing off at the heel strengthens the calf muscles and the hamstrings along the back of the leg. Extending the leg in the forward stride tones the quadriceps in the front of the thigh; the hip flexors and buttocks muscles are worked by lengthening your stride. In addition, fitness walking conditions the abdominals, and swinging the arms works the arm and shoulder muscles.

Proper posture is very important to effective walking: you should stand straight with your shoulders back but relaxed. Your arms should move in opposition to your legs *(opposite)*. Plant your feet almost in front of each other, as if you were walking along an imaginary line.

Do some simple stretching exercises both before and after your workout to warm up and cool down.

On impact, plant your foot so that your heel lands first at about a 90-degree angle to your leg and a 45-degree angle to the ground *(above)*. Rock forwards as your trailing foot begins to lift off the ground *(centre)*. Roll forwards on your back foot to push off the ground with your toes and complete the stride *(right)*.

Reaching for Higher Intensity

As your walking programme progresses, your cardiovascular system will become more efficient, so that, even when you are walking as fast as you comfortably can, you will have difficulty reaching your target heart rate. This is an indication that you require to intensify your walking.

One of the best ways to increase the effort and the benefits of walking is to incorporate hill work *(right)*. Walking up a 10 degree incline can almost double the energy costs of walking the same distance on level ground; steeper gradients increase the effort further. Lean forwards slightly when walking uphill and swing your arms vigorously.

Walking downhill requires more effort than walking on level ground but less effort than walking uphill. The extra work of downhill walking is due to the exertion required to brake your acceleration.

Carrying weights as you walk is another effective way of making your workout more demanding. You will receive the greatest benefit from combining hand weights with vigorous arm swings *(see chart, page 16)*. This combination will result in an energy expenditure that is comparable to slow jogging. (If you have back problems, you should probably avoid using hand weights.) Begin with 0.5 kilogram weights and work up to 1.5 kilograms.

A final way to add both variety and intensity to your walking is to vary the terrain. When you walk on a beach, the resistance offered by sand increases energy output by almost a third. Hiking is even more strenuous; you may expend 50 per cent more energy walking on a rough trail than you would on a road.

Pump your arms as you do in forward walking. Extend your arms slightly to the sides to aid in balance.

Retro Walking

Retro, or backward, movement is commonly used in many sports, such as soccer, basketball and tennis. Recently it has gained acceptance as a means of injury rehabilitation. In addition, it aids in achieving muscle balance by strengthening opposing muscles.

Studies have shown that retro walking is not merely the mirror image of forward walking; indeed, there are very distinct biomechanical differences in body position and the use of the legs. The greatest difference is in the action of the knee joint. Retro walking affords the knee an increased range of motion, which results in a greater stretch of the hamstrings. The range of motion required in the hip joint is decreased in retro walking, which places less stress on the hip muscles. Furthermore, preliminary studies indicate that the energy expenditure of backward movement is far greater than that of forward movement.

You can incorporate up to 400 metres of retro walking into your walking workout; this is sufficient to give you its unique benefits. Bear in mind that retro walking does have a drawback — the danger of bumping into something or falling down. You should never perform retro walking on a street. A track is ideal, but any smooth surface without traffic will do. Periodically check to see what is behind you by looking over your shoulder — alternate shoulders to prevent neck cramping — or walk with a partner who moves forwards as you walk backwards.

In retro walking, the push-off phase is accomplished with the heel of your forward foot *(left)*. The leg then swings back and lands on the forefoot *(above)*.

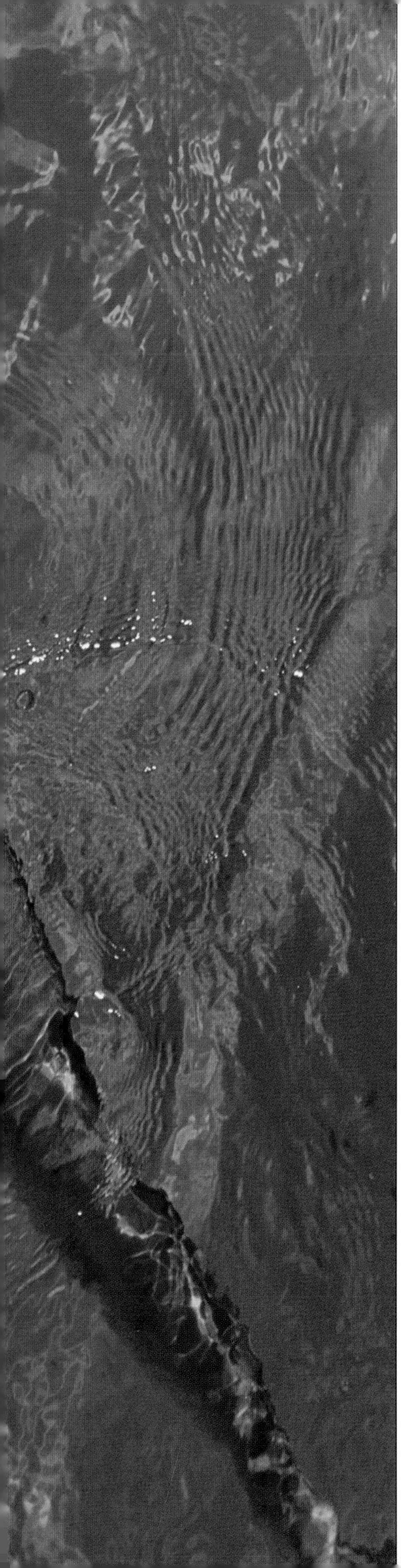

Chapter Three

Water Workouts

Versatile routines in a virtually stress-free environment

Swimming is often considered an ideal exercise because of its superlative conditioning benefits coupled with low rates of injury. But non-swimming water workouts can incorporate many of these benefits, and can even work some additional muscles not used in swimming. A carefully designed water exercise regimen can be a comprehensive programme that targets all four major areas of fitness: flexibility, co-ordination, strength and endurance. And if you swim in an indoor pool you can work out year round and compensate for having to curtail other seasonal exercises.

The buoyancy of water makes it an ideal medium for injury-free exercise, while the resistance it supplies can build and tone muscles. Buoyancy, the upward pressure that water exerts to help keep you afloat, effectively reduces a person's body weight by 90 per cent. For example, the feet and legs of a 68-kilogram man in water up to his neck have to support only 7 kilograms. This apparent decrease in weight means that less stress is placed on joints and ligaments. An impetus for the development of water workouts has been the success of hydrotherapy, or rehabilitation in water following injury, which often returns damaged joints and muscles to full usage and restores range of motion more quickly than other types of physiotherapy.

The buoyancy of water also makes it an especially good exercise environment for handicapped, overweight or pregnant individuals for whom weight-bearing exercise is difficult. But water workouts can benefit anyone who exercises, from beginners to professional athletes. Indeed, many coaches are now incorporating pool workouts into their teams' training programmes. In an effort to cut back on the injuries sustained in competitive cross-country running, the coach of Yale University's cross-country team recently eliminated one of the team's two daily workouts on land and substituted running in deep water. Although the runners' weekly distance dropped from between 95 and 110 kilometres to between 70 and 80 kilometres, the team had a winning — and virtually injury-free — season. Overall, water workouts reduced stress injuries by 90 per cent.

Water running is one of many pool exercises that are simply land exercises performed in water. Research has shown that such exercises translated into a water medium can provide benefits to the heart, lungs and circulation comparable to the same exercises done on land. One university study compared the cardiovascular effects of water and land running in 16 runners. Half the group trained as usual, while the rest ran in deep water, using flotation devices to maintain an upright posture. The water runners showed no significant decrease in VO_2max, an important gauge of cardiovascular fitness that measures the ability of a person to take in and use oxygen.

The resistance of water, which is about 800 times heavier than air, makes exercising in it very effective for muscle development; this resistance means that an exercise performed in the water requires more effort than the same exercise done on land. For example, if you run a kilometre in five minutes on dry land, it will take you just under 20 minutes to run the same distance in waist-high water. And the deeper the water, the more difficult the exercise. One study of walking in water found that water depth was a significant factor in the metabolic costs of the activity. Using a submerged treadmill, researchers measured oxygen consumption in 11 subjects at a range of walking speeds and at varying water depths. Walkers at all water depths showed significantly higher VO_2max than those walking on land. Interestingly, another study found that the metabolic costs of water walking are more than twice as great as land walking, although the energy costs of both land and water running are essentially the same. Researchers attribute this fact to the difficulty of maintaining proper running form in the water.

Water resistance is also exerted evenly in all directions. This constant pressure makes water ideal for strengthening exercises because it works opposing muscle groups equally. By contrast, most weight-training is based on resistance to gravity and works one muscle group

Getting Started

◆ One important factor in effective water workouts is your choice of swimming pool. Try to find one with a bottom that slopes gradually, allowing you to stand in water up to your waist at one point, and your shoulders at another. A gutter or swim trough round the perimeter will allow you to perform certain exercises that require gripping an edge or hoisting yourself out of the water. For some exercises, holding on to the top rung of a pool ladder will suffice.

◆ Aquatic equipment can enhance or intensify your workout. Flotation vests provide support for water running and walking; they also allow you to work out in deep water if you are a non-swimmer. Kickboards let you practise your swim kicks. Hand paddles provide extra resistance for arm work; fins do the same for your legs.

◆ The pool and its environs should be well maintained. Though cloudy pool water does not necessarily imply that upkeep is substandard, the proper chemical balance is important for your health. Check with an attendant if you have any doubts. As a rule, if the water is clear enough for you to see the drain at the deep end, the pool is sufficiently clean.

◆ Good posture is essential for the effective performance of many of the water workouts demonstrated in this chapter. If you keep your abdomen and buttocks muscles tucked in as you exercise, you will avoid the pressure on lower back muscles that overarching your back can cause. Be sure that you remain relaxed as you go through each exercise sequence.

at a time, leaving open the possibility that opposing muscle groups will not get equivalent workouts.

The resistance of water can be controlled: the more you push against it, the more it will resist. Adjusting the speed at which you perform a particular motion will vary the resistance and thus your energy expenditure. Furthermore, the constant resistance encountered in water means that virtually any type of exercise includes a strengthening element. For example, the leg stretches on pages 82-83 are basically flexibility exercises, but on account of the water resistance, these exercises also strengthen the muscles of the legs.

Because almost all the exercises in this chapter can be performed while standing in the water, you need not be a swimmer to get the benefits of these workouts. However, the naturally low-impact benefits of swimming can intensify your workout. A number of the exercises that follow isolate various swimming motions — the arm movement that is used in the breaststroke or the leg motion in the flutter kick, for example. Non-swimmers can perform these exercises at the side of the pool or holding on to a kickboard to attain some of the specific muscular and cardiovascular benefits of swimming. Of course, if you enjoy swimming, you are encouraged to add this activity to your low-impact exercise regimen.

A Complete Routine

The comprehensive workout on the following 14 pages is divided into three sections: strengtheners, stretches for flexibility and aerobics. The swimming movements on pages 90-95 enhance co-ordination, thus rounding out a fitness programme.

Ideally you should work out in a pool with a water temperature of between 29 and 32 degrees Celsius. You may be more comfortable performing routines that call for relatively more exertion in water that is between 28 and 30 degrees Celsius.

The natural cooling effect of water coupled with its buoyancy means that you might not be fully aware of the workload your muscles are subjected to, but a water workout can be just as intense as a land-based regimen. Therefore, you should devote a minimum of five minutes to the warm-ups on these two pages to prepare your muscles for exertion; after your workout, spend at least five minutes on cool-downs *(pages 96-97)*. Perform each of the following exercises 10 times or for one minute if it is a continuous activity such as running. Increase these repetitions gradually as you become more conditioned. Work towards 20 to 30 repetitions or three to five minutes of continuous activity.

Also, be sure to drink plenty of water both before and after you exercise in a pool: even though you may not realize it, you perspire when you exercise in water, particularly during an aerobic workout.

Stand in chest-high water. Walk round the pool, keeping the same form you would use if you were walking on land: hold your head high and do not lean too far forwards. Swing your arms as you alternate legs.

Stand erect in chest-high water with your arms at your sides. Keeping your back straight, flex your knees and lower yourself until the water is at shoulder level. Bend your elbows and extend your arms for support. Bob.

Strengtheners/1

Stand in water up to your neck with your feet spread. Extend your arms from your sides at about a 45-degree angle and rotate them in small circles *(left)*. Then raise your arms to shoulder height and rotate them in small circles *(below)*.

Stand at arm's length from the edge of the pool in chest-high water. Spread your feet slightly and hold on to the edge with your hands *(opposite)*. Keep your back straight as you bend your arms and lean inwards to bring your chin up to the edge *(inset, left)*. Push out to return to the original position, then push off on your feet, straightening your arms to hold you against the side of the pool with your upper body out of the water *(inset, right)*.

Strengtheners/2

For an aquatic version of a sit-up, place your back against a corner of the pool, using your outstretched arms for support. Tuck your knees into your chest *(above)*, then forcefully push your legs straight out so that they are parallel to the pool bottom *(top)*.

For this more difficult sit-up variation, support yourself with your outstretched arms, this time along a straight side of the pool. Tuck your legs into your chest *(below)*, then push them straight out from your hips *(bottom)*.

Strengtheners/3

Stand in shoulder-deep water with your feet together and your hands at your sides *(left)*. Jump, simultaneously spreading your legs and raising your arms to just below shoulder height *(below)*. Jump and return to the original position.

Stand in shoulder-deep water with your feet slightly spread and your arms outstretched. Swing your arms round as you twist your torso first to the left *(above)*, then to the right. Put your hands on your hips and twist to your right and then to your left *(right)*.

Stretches/1

Stand at arm's length from the edge of the pool in waist-high water. Hold on to the edge with your right hand and place your left hand at your waist. Lift your left leg sideways to hip height *(opposite)*. Bring it forwards, again at hip height *(left)*, then raise it backwards *(below)*. Reverse sides and repeat.

You will need a pool with steps for this exercise. Place your right foot on the bottom step and lean forwards. Reverse legs.

Stretches/2

Stand with the balls of your feet on the bottom step of the pool stairs; hold on to the pool edge with your hand. Let your heels drop down; hold momentarily. Rise back up and repeat.

Hold on to the edge of the pool and stand an arm's length away. Place your right foot on a step that is about thigh high. Extend your right leg and lean forwards over it. Repeat with your left leg.

Aerobics/1

Stand in waist-deep water and run backwards. Keep your back straight and pump your arms as you run.

Run forwards in waist-deep water. Hold your chest high and pump your arms to maintain an upright position.

In addition to being a life-saving skill, treading water is a good aerobic exercise that can be sustained for long periods. Perform this exercise in neck-deep water until you are comfortable and then move to tread water out of your depth. Pump your legs continuously as if you were on a bicycle; repeatedly extend your arms *(left)*, then bend your elbows to cross them in front of your chest *(below)*.

Aerobics/2

Stand in chest-deep water and link your hands behind your head. Bend your left knee and lift your leg to hip height as you twist your torso, bringing your right elbow to your raised knee *(right)*. Drop your left knee and bring up your right, touching it to your left elbow *(below)*.

Stand in shoulder-deep water with your elbows bent at your sides. Rotate your wrists and jump up and down as if you were twirling a skipping rope.

Swimming Manoeuvres/1

A total water workout should include swimming. Not only is swimming a most effective cardiovascular conditioner and an excellent muscle toner, but it can also contribute the rather important elements of co-ordination and agility to your fitness programme.

The exercises on these two pages and the following four isolate some of the arm and leg motions used in swimming. Concentrating individually on these specific manoeuvres will help you to perfect them, as well as condition the muscles used in swimming. Perform each of the strokes and kicks for at least one minute. Then combine them and add about 15 minutes, or more, of length swimming to your water workout.

BUTTERFLY STROKE Stand in neck-deep water. Move your arms simultaneously, each arm curving outwards, then inwards to your sides as they enter the water. Follow this by using alternate arms to make an S-shape pull, which is the front crawl stroke.

SIDESTROKE Stand in neck-deep water. Turn your head so that it tilts to the right side and tuck your arms in front of your chest with your hands cupped outwards *(left)*. Move your arms in opposite motions, one arm pulling and one pushing; push backwards with your left arm, letting your right arm glide forwards *(bottom)*. Then pull towards your chest with your right arm as your left arm glides back to your chest. Tilt your head to the left and repeat for your left side.

Swimming Manoeuvres/2

BREASTSTROKE Bend your arms so that your hands touch and point forwards in front of your chest *(left)*. Move your hands forwards, then gradually separate your hands, cupping them to push the water away from you *(below)*. Extend your arms out to your sides *(bottom)*, then bend your elbows and bring them back into your chest in a heart-shaped motion.

This exercise uses water resistance to build up the arm strength necessary for effective swimming strokes. Spread your legs and forcefully punch the water in front of you, alternating arms.

FLUTTER KICK You can either use a kickboard or hold on to the edge of the pool to practise kicking movements. Stretch your legs out straight behind you with your ankles relaxed and your toes pointed. Alternately kick your legs, letting the motion come from your hip *(above)*.

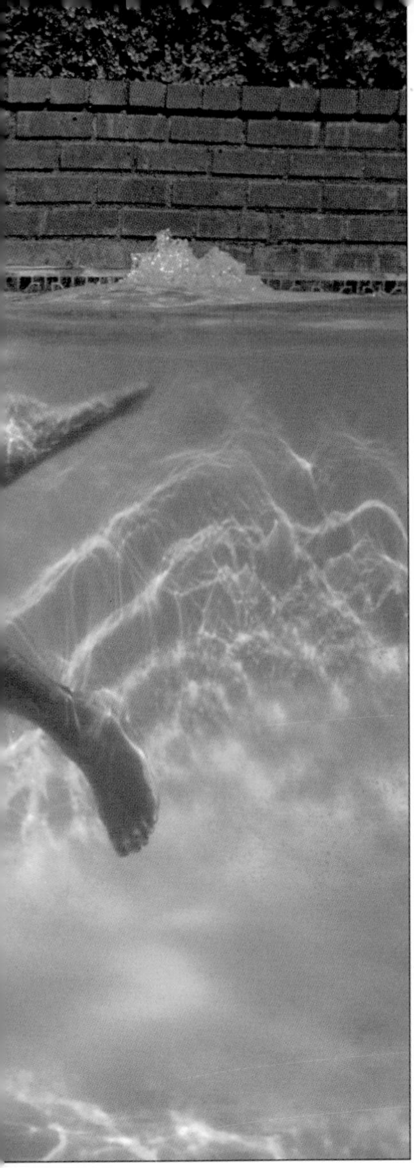

Swimming Manoeuvres/3

SCISSORS KICK Hold on to a kickboard and support yourself sideways in the water. Begin with your legs together and your toes pointed. Bring your knees towards your chest, then back down as you separate and straighten your legs in a wide V shape *(above)*. Then bring your legs back together.

Cool-Downs

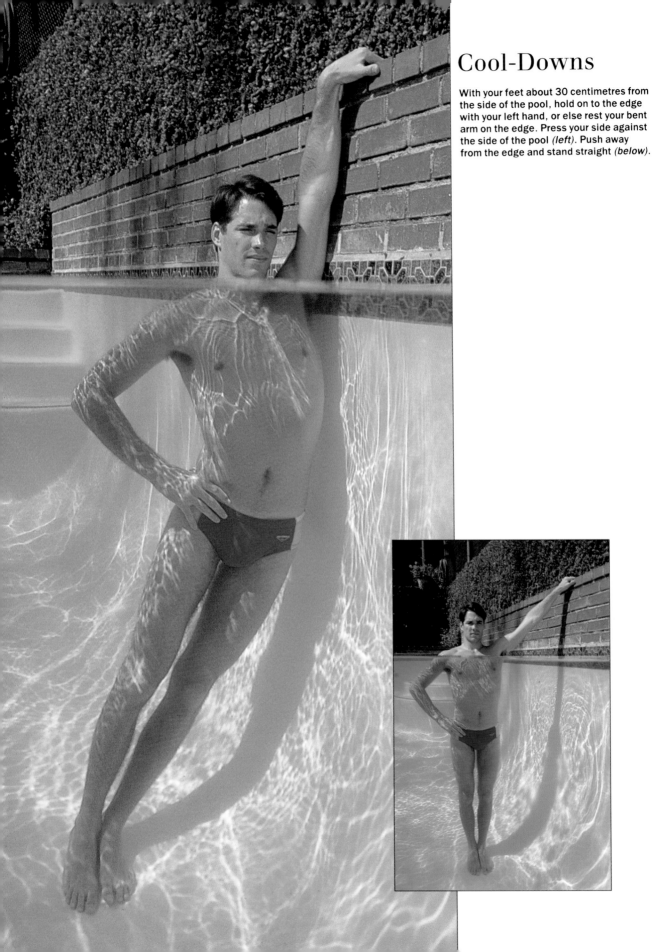

With your feet about 30 centimetres from the side of the pool, hold on to the edge with your left hand, or else rest your bent arm on the edge. Press your side against the side of the pool *(left)*. Push away from the edge and stand straight *(below)*.

If your pool has a bar, grip it; otherwise, hold on to the gutter. Bring your feet up against the side of the pool just beneath your hands and extend your arms and legs. Hold.

Stand in waist-deep water. Hold a rolled towel at either end and bend to your left *(top)*, then to your right *(right)*.

CHAPTER FOUR

Movement

Low-impact routines for developing your natural grace and agility

One of the best ways of softening the impact of any exercise is to take advantage of the body's natural movement patterns. Understanding what happens to your body when you undertake physical activity is the basis for movement theory, whose proponents have developed special motion sequences in order to improve co-ordination, flexibility and agility.

The scientific underpinning of movement theory is kinesiology, which draws on the physical sciences — particularly physics, anatomy and physiology — to examine the ways in which human bodies move. By applying to the body the mechanical principles of balance, equilibrium and the application of force, kinesiologists try to explain the operational requirements of motion.

Kinesiologists view the body as a machine whose movements are co-ordinated and can be mapped. For example, a kinesiologist will determine how the laws of motion apply to the activity of running in order to understand the mechanics of acceleration and forward propulsion. Comprehending which mechanisms control the body's operation and how they do it can be a means to revising ineffective movement patterns. This enables the kinesiologist to create an ideal model for running that can be used to improve an individual runner's technique.

Like kinesiologists, movement therapists seek to understand how individual muscles and parts of the body function within the context of the whole system. However, they do not study the body through the biomechanical lens of the kinesiologist. While both kinesiologists and movement therapists base their suggestions for improvements on their analysis of a subject, movement therapists view this process as educational as well as diagnostic. Thus, they encourage the individual to examine his or her movement patterns from another perspective — an internal one. Such an analysis requires that the individual develop an awareness of not only his or her bodily sensations, but also how he or she uses the surrounding space.

Much of the graceful motion associated with childhood is lost as you grow older, when you may find yourself forced into standing or sitting for prolonged periods. To counteract this, movement therapists make use of routines that re-create the development of gross motor skills in the human body. By imitating the progression of human physical development from lying down to rolling over, standing, pivoting and walking, movement sequences can help to improve the performance of basic activities.

Any time the body moves, there is a primary and usually intentional action coupled with secondary, or complementary actions, usually meant to balance the body. The primary muscular action of throwing a ball, for example, occurs in the throwing arm. Secondary actions in the legs and torso maintain the body's balance. Movement therapists treat every bodily function as part of a comprehensive effort. For example, although a sit-up is primarily an exercise for the abdominals, it requires the co-ordinated effort of your back, head, arms and legs. Movement therapists claim that such exercise performed without an understanding of the interactions of the entire body can be ineffectual and sometimes dangerous. Thus, they do not prescribe exercises for single body parts. Rather, they create sequences that require concentration on the secondary action as well as on the primary action. Performing sequences such as the walk-around on pages 120-121, which emphasizes the proper alignment between the head and the pelvis, and the roundabout on pages 114-115, which necessitates complementary use of leg and abdominal muscles, will develop your awareness of the careful body co-ordination that is required for even a relatively simple motion.

In the movement sequences on the following eight pages, the entire routines are performed in a standing, sitting or kneeling position. When you become proficient at these, you can progress to the more advanced sequences, starting on page 110, that incorporate the element of transition — shifting from sitting to standing and sometimes back to the floor — and so require working with gravity. Routines

Movement Fundamentals

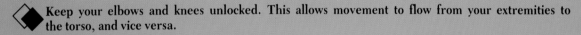

◆ **Maintain a slight contraction of your abdominal muscles.** These muscles provide support for both your upper and lower body and help forces generated in the lower body to be transferred to the upper body and vice versa; for example, the arm movement for throwing a ball is initiated by taking a step, and contracted abdominals will aid in this transfer of force. Contracted abdominals also help protect your lower body from overuse and strain. The roundabout *(pages 114-115)* is strongly dependent on this principle for its successful execution.

◆ **Co-ordinate your breathing with exertion.** As part of the mechanism of breathing, exhaling facilitates the contraction of your abdominal muscles. The spider *(pages 110-111)* is a good exercise to practise this technique with.

◆ **Strive for full rotation of the hip and shoulder joints.** These ball-and-socket joints are designed to move in a full circular range, and mobility in the hip and shoulder can prevent lower back or neck strain. Ineffective movement patterns frequently substitute use of the lower back, knees and neck for movement that ought to occur in the hip or shoulder. To facilitate full range of motion in the shoulder, turn your palm upwards when you move your arm in front of you; when you move your arm behind you, turn the palm downwards. Practise arm rotations in the serve *(pages 106-107)* and the cantilever *(pages 122-123)*. To enhance hip rotation, turn the inside of your thigh upwards when moving your leg forwards, and downwards towards the floor when moving your leg backwards. Both leg-threading *(pages 102-103)* and the crawl-around *(pages 108-109)* rely on full hip rotation.

◆ **Move your upper and lower body in opposing directions to maintain balance.** This important principle, called counterbalance, establishes equilibrium in motion. Balance is not static; for instance, as your arm moves forwards, one of your legs will move back. Counterbalance can be maintained in many different configurations: up and down, the basic balancing movement you use when getting up from a chair and which is used in the walk-around *(pages 120-121)*; forwards and backwards, seen in the cantilever *(pages 122-123)*; side to side, a movement in the figure-of-eight *(pages 116-117)*; and diagonal counterbalance, demonstrated in the crossover *(pages 112-113)*.

◆ **Keep your elbows and knees unlocked.** This allows movement to flow from your extremities to the torso, and vice versa.

such as the side circling on pages 118-119 require careful balance and co-ordination to complete the transitions successfully.

The movement skills you will acquire from these sequences can be used to improve other activities or exercises. For example, the throw and the serve sequences on pages 106-107 are designed to duplicate use of the muscles in baseball, rounders and racket sports. In addition, all of the sequences encourage full joint mobility, which in turn allows muscles to work more efficiently. This can significantly reduce the effort — and possible injury — inherent in many forms of exercise. Many athletic strains and injuries result from overuse of the neck, lower back and knees because of a lack of shoulder and hip-joint mobility. The sequences in this chapter encourage the full use of these joints, thus distributing the stress on the body more evenly.

1

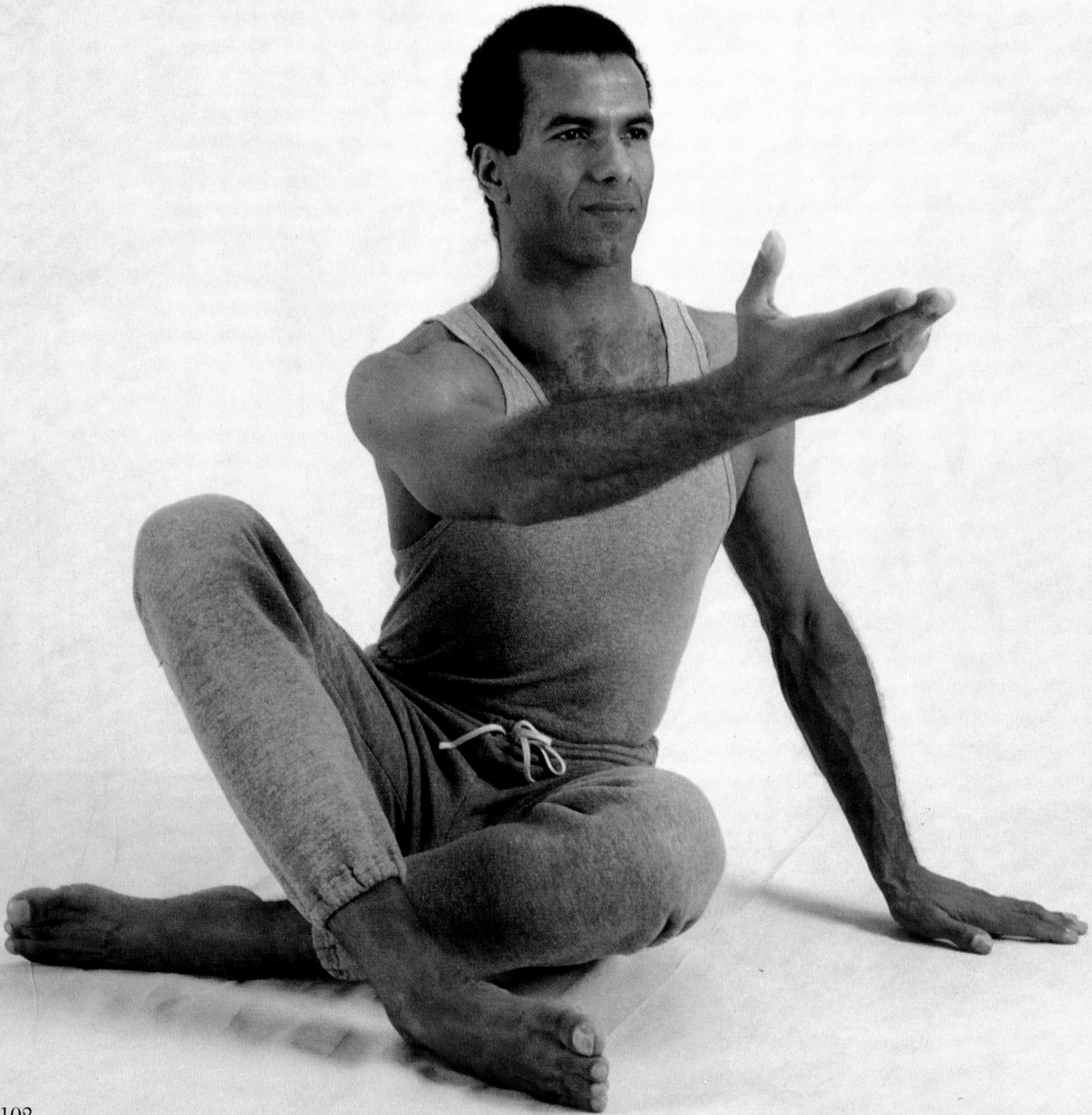

2

The Basic Routines

The goal of movement routines is not to build strength or endurance through increased repetitions or longer workouts, as many exercise programmes aim to do. Instead, the object is to develop an understanding of the interactions among parts of the body. Many of the following routines, for example, emphasize co-ordination of the head with the pelvis. These separate body parts must function interdependently to help ensure proper posture.

Mastering such techniques can also help you improve your performance in many other physical endeavours. Initiating leg movement with hip-joint rotation, as the routine on these two pages does, can give you further insight into the biomechanical requirements for activities such as kicking a football or doing the breaststroke — both of which use the hip joint.

To benefit from these routines, you should practise them slowly and precisely; only in that way can you become aware of the co-ordination of your body in movement.

The following five sequences are relatively simple because each is confined to one basic posture: sitting, standing, kneeling or lying. Work on a mat or a thick carpet.

You should aim for smooth, flowing motion from step to step. Performing the routines in front of a mirror might help you to evaluate your movements.

Perform each routine two or three times. And with sequences that are shown for only one side of the body, be sure to repeat them on the other side as well.

LEG THREADING Sit cross-legged on the floor. Support yourself with your left arm as you raise your right knee and extend your right arm in front of you (1). Rotate your right arm and right leg to the right side (2). Curve your outstretched arm downwards, as you bend your right knee up (3). Thread your right foot under your left leg and return your right arm to its original position (4).

Windmill

1

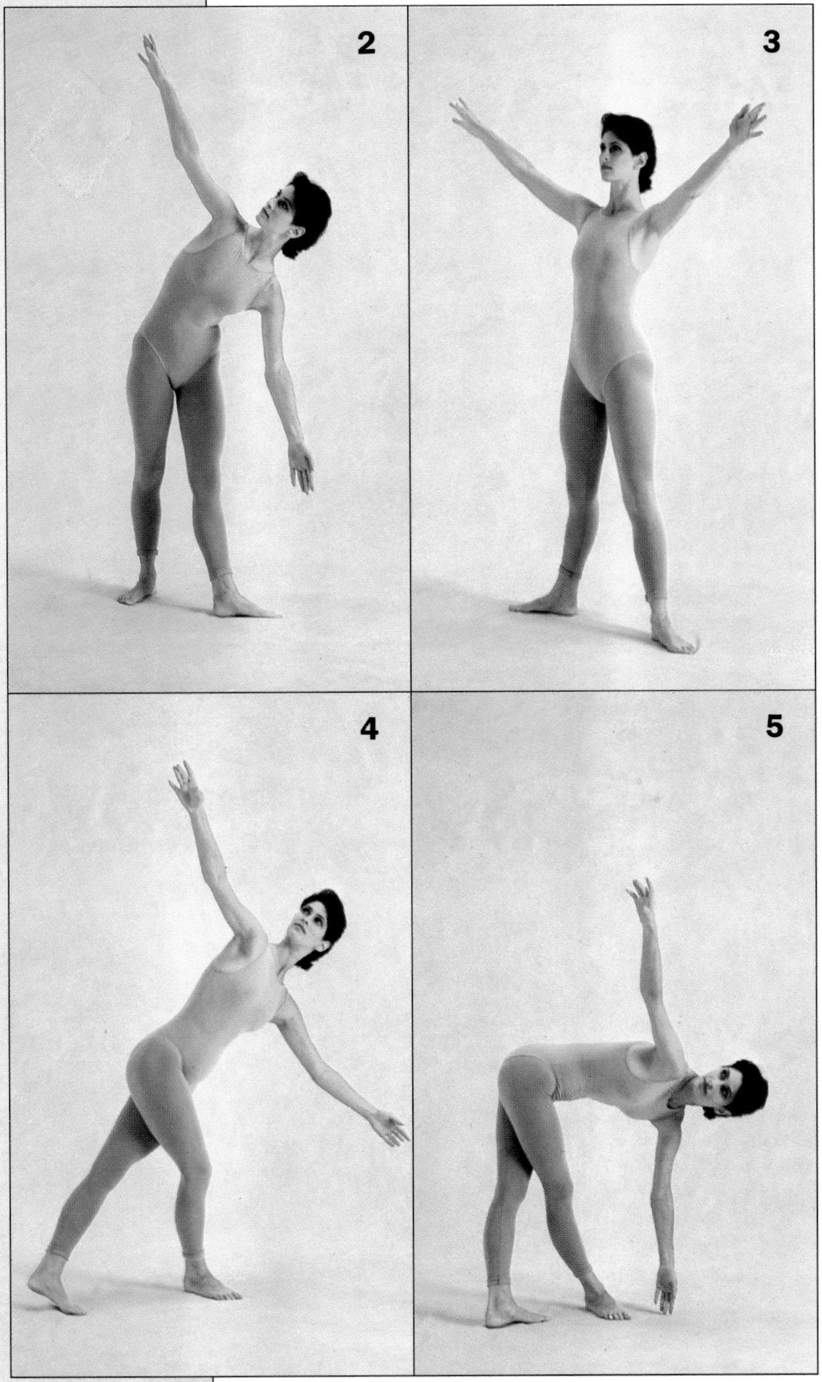

Stand with your feet spread slightly and at right angles to each other, your left foot in front. Lean forwards to touch the floor in front of your left foot with the fingertips of your left hand, keeping both arms fully extended, with your right arm above you (1). Slowly unbend and reach your right arm upwards (2), rising to an erect posture with arms outstretched and feet spread (3). Pivot 180 degrees on your right foot, bringing your left foot behind you (4), then bend over to touch the floor with your left hand. Your right arm should extend upwards again (5). This exercise should not be attempted by anyone who has lower back problems.

Throw

Stand up straight, then lean on to your right leg, letting your left foot lift slightly, and reach up with your right arm (1). Bring your left foot forwards and lean back on your right leg, dropping your arm (2). Then shift your weight on to your left leg as you curve your right arm forwards and raise your right leg behind you (3).

Serve

Stand with your feet spread wide and your arms outstretched. Bend your right knee slightly and lean to the right (1). Lean backwards, moving your right leg and right arm back, and extend your left arm in front of you (2). Thrust your right arm forwards smoothly, lifting your right leg as you shift your weight on to your left (3).

Crawl-Around

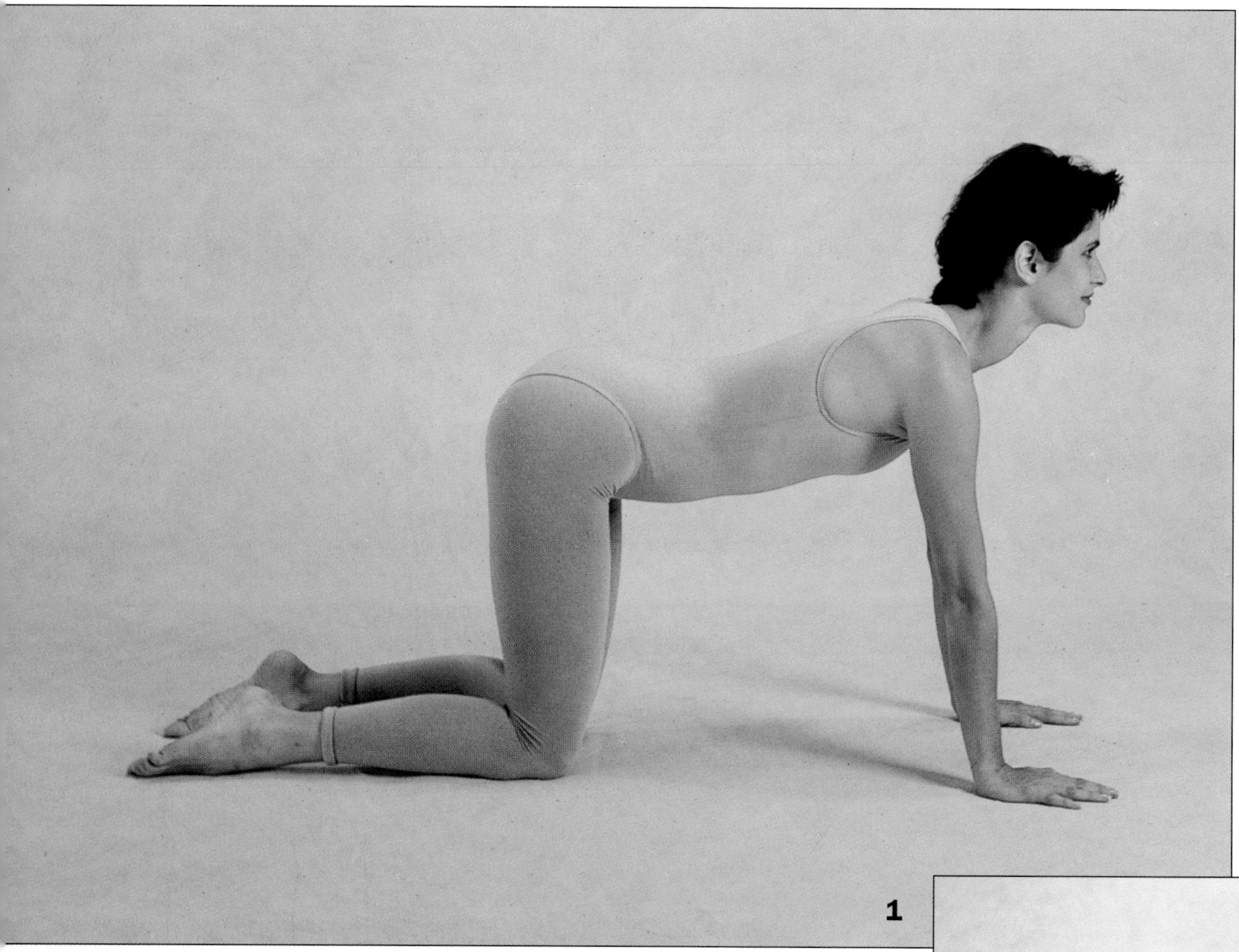

1

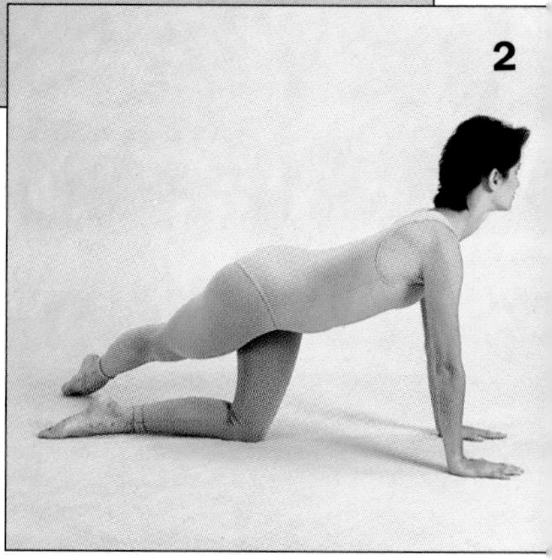

2

Kneel on all fours, keeping your back flat (1). Extend your right leg, crossing it over your left (2). Swing the right leg out to your right side so that it forms a right angle when you bend your knee (3). Cross your right leg in front of your left and drop the knee to the floor (4). Raise your left leg and bring it over the right and return to the starting position (5).

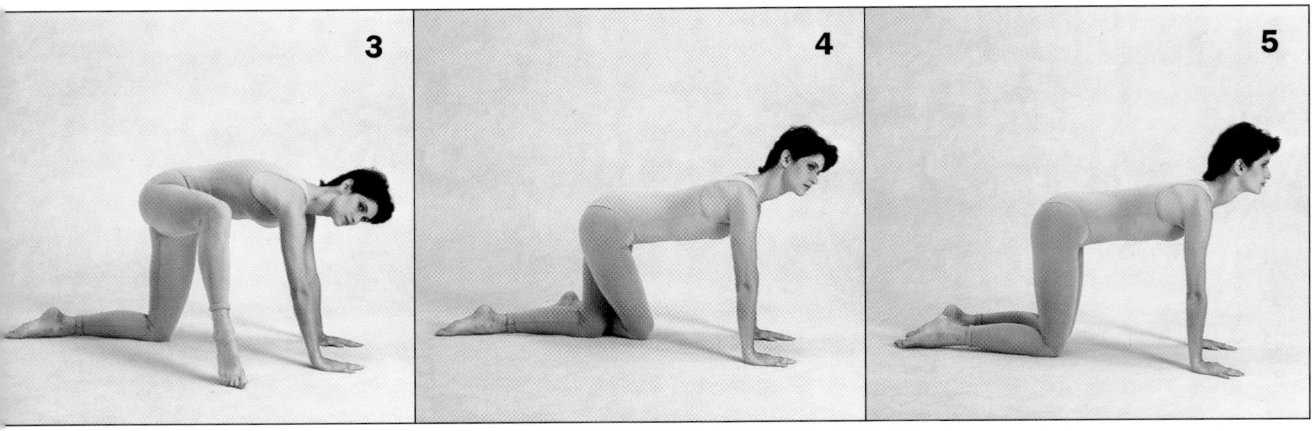

Adding Transitions

Once you have mastered the sequences demonstrated on pages 102-109, you are ready to move on to more advanced routines. These include transitions that call for you to shift postures from standing to sitting to lying. The shifts in position mean that you have to compensate for the pull of gravity — for example, propulsion is necessary to push off on one leg and stand up from a kneeling position, and momentum is needed to roll up from a lying to a sitting posture.

Do not try to perform all these routines immediately. Concentrate on perfecting two or three exercises before working on a new one.

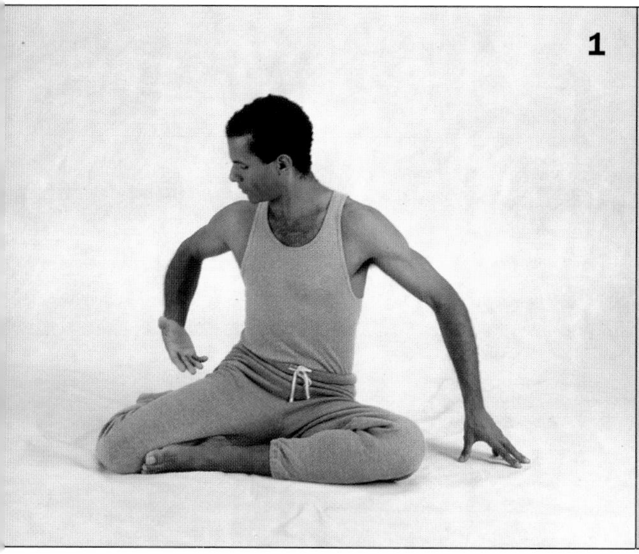

SPIDER Sit with your left leg bent in front of you and your right leg bent back at the knee. Support yourself on your left arm and curve your right arm (1). Bring your right arm forwards as you extend your right leg back (2). Cross your right leg in front of you and reach your right arm behind you (3), then, supporting yourself on your hands in front of you, shift your weight forwards on to your bent right leg and extend your left leg behind you (4). Shift your weight from your right to your left leg through a squatting position (5), extending your right leg sideways (6). Pivot your hips to fold your right knee underneath you (7). Continue turning to lower yourself to a seated position with your left leg bent across your right (8). Circle your left leg to the side and bend it behind you (9).

Crossover

Lie flat on your back with your arms and legs outstretched (1). Reach your left arm across your body to roll on to your right side (2), then to a prone position (3). Reach your right leg behind you to roll to your left, simultaneously pushing up with your arms (4), then twist to a sitting position with your right leg extended and your left leg folded in front of you (5). Turn your torso over your right leg, and extend your arms in front of you (6). Keep twisting your torso to the right, extending your legs behind you and supporting yourself on your arms as you roll again to a prone position (7). Extend your arms to push your torso up and turn to your left (8), rising to sit with your right leg folded in front and your left leg and your right arm extended (9).

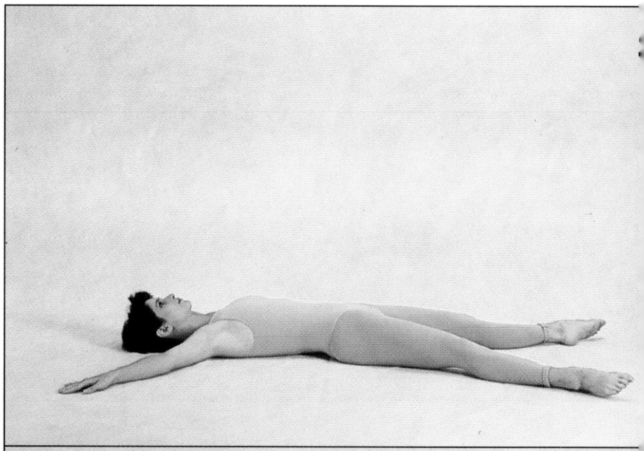

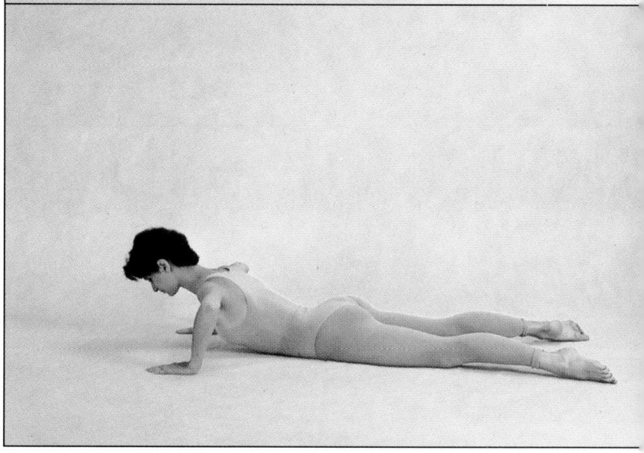

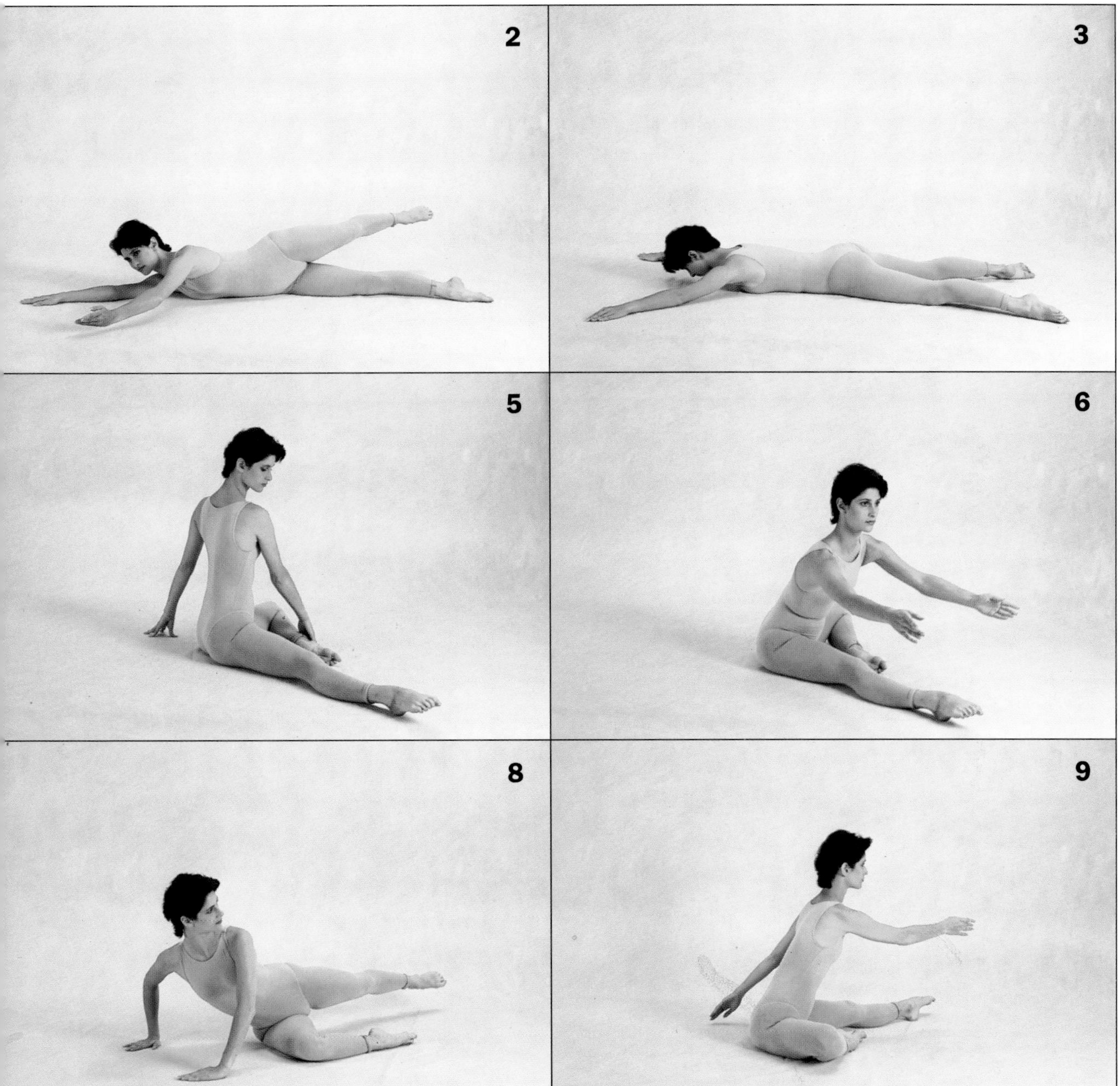
2
3
5
6
8
9

Roundabout

Lean on your arms with your legs outstretched to your left (1). Lift your left arm and pivot on to your hip (2) to swing your legs directly in front of you, keeping your feet slightly raised off the floor (3). Continue pivoting and moving your legs, shifting your weight to your left arm (4), then twisting your body forwards on to both arms (5), as your legs rotate behind you (6). Straighten your arms as you cross your right leg, knee bent, behind you (7). Continue turning your torso until you sit facing the opposite direction from where you began (8).

1

2

5

6

3

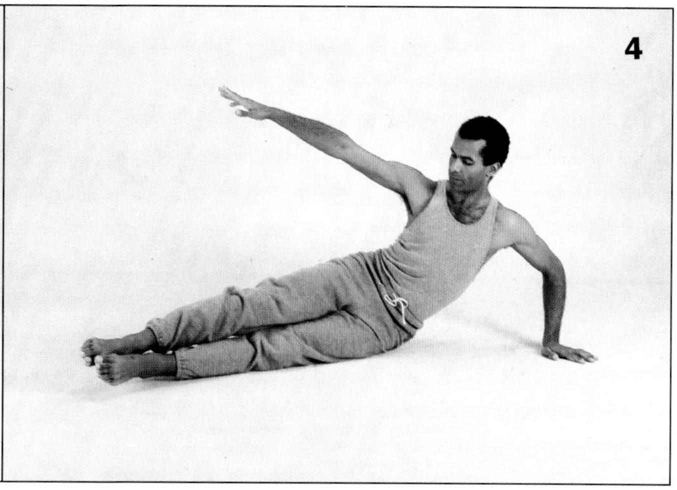

4

7

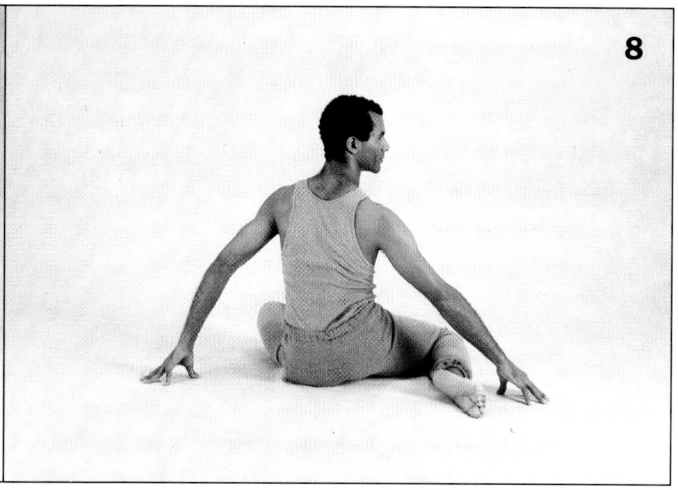

8

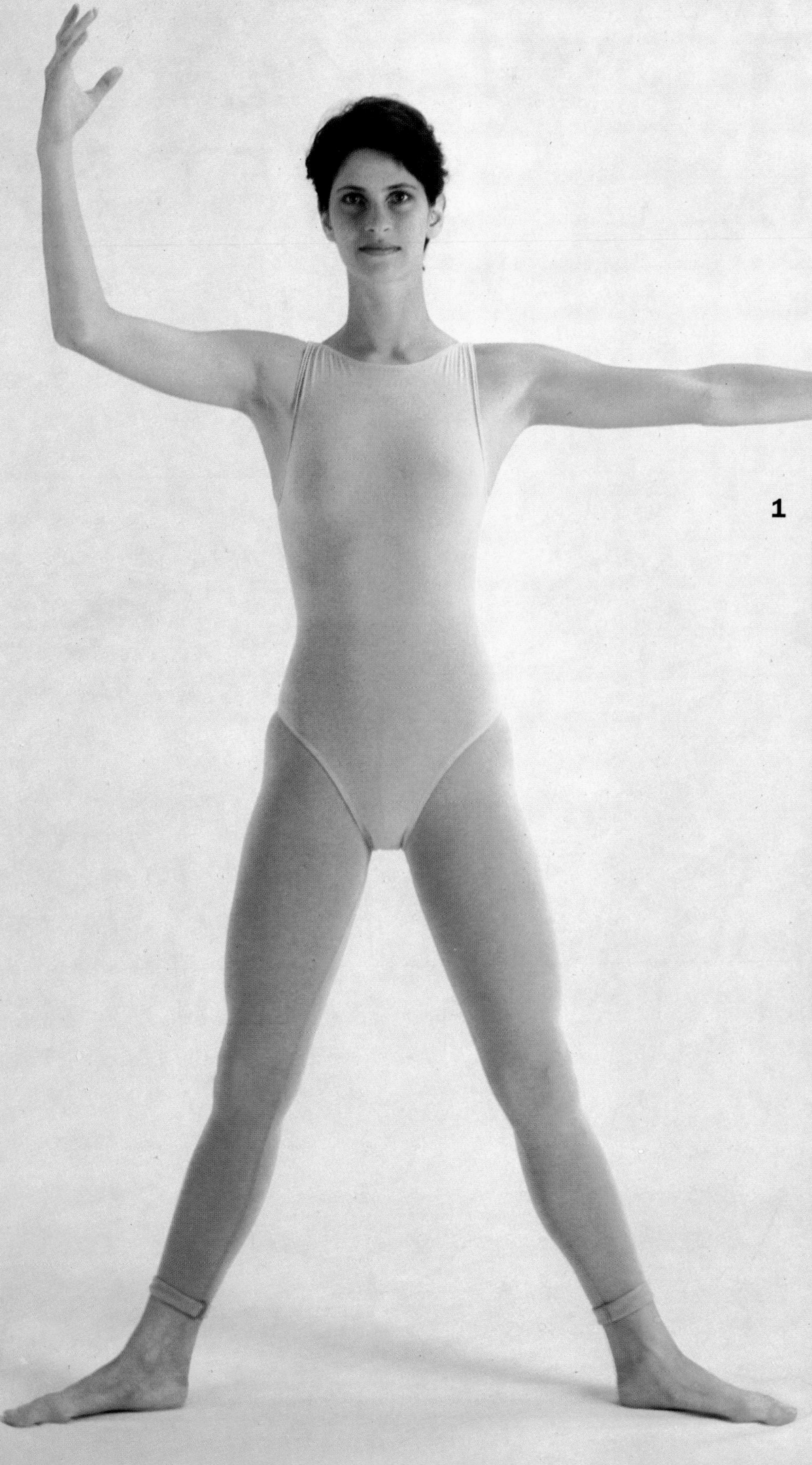

1

2

6

Figure-of-Eight

Stand with your feet spread apart, your left arm extended and your right arm bent at the elbow (1). Shift your weight to the left, crossing your right arm in front of you (2), then bend both knees (3) and swing both your arms to the right, allowing your torso to shift over your right leg (4). Keep rotating your arms to the right as you bend your left knee (5) and fold yourself into a cross-legged sit (6). Next, swing your arms to the left and unfold your legs (7), pivoting on your right leg (8). Centre your weight as you rise to your original position (9).

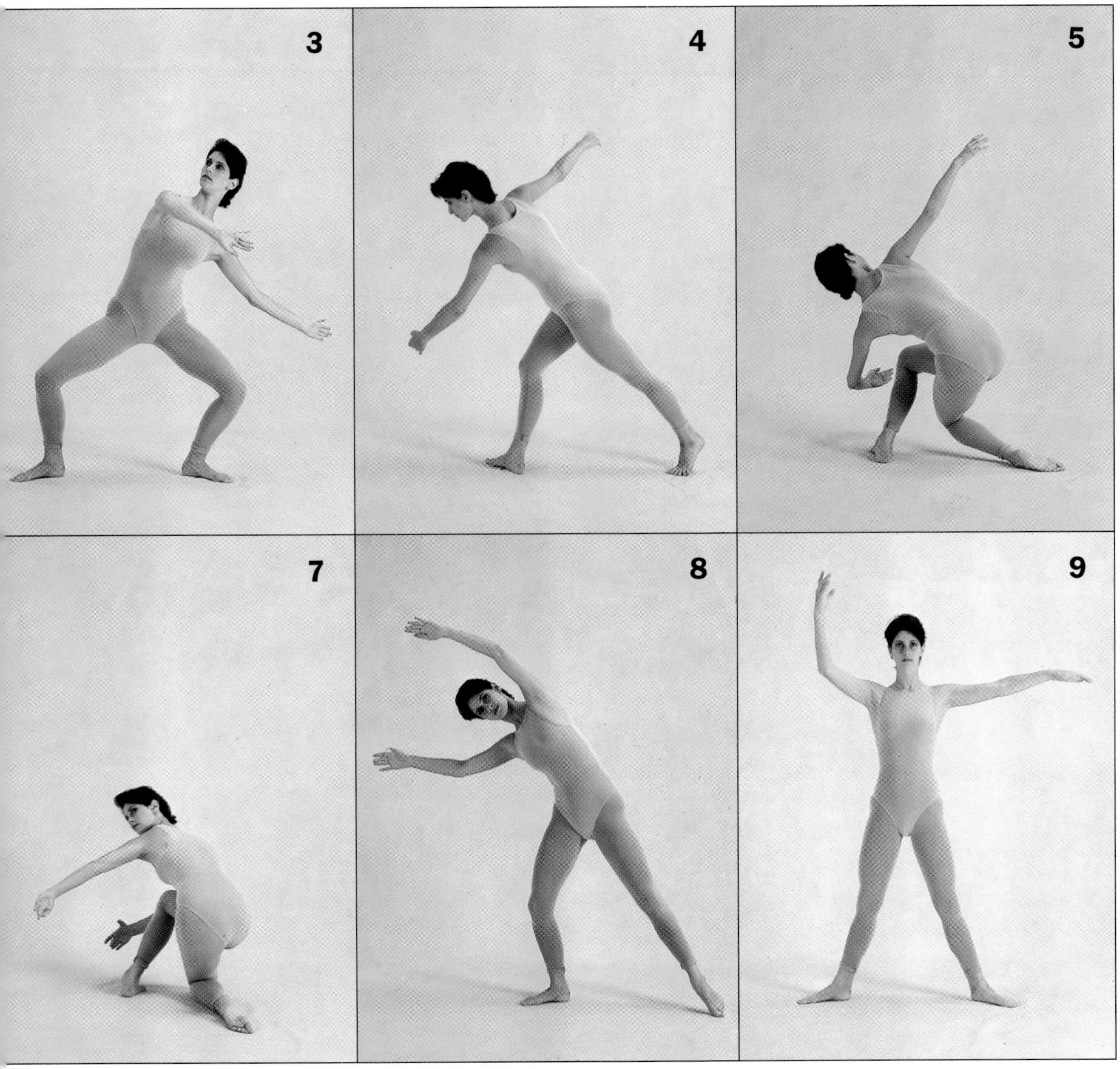

Side Circling

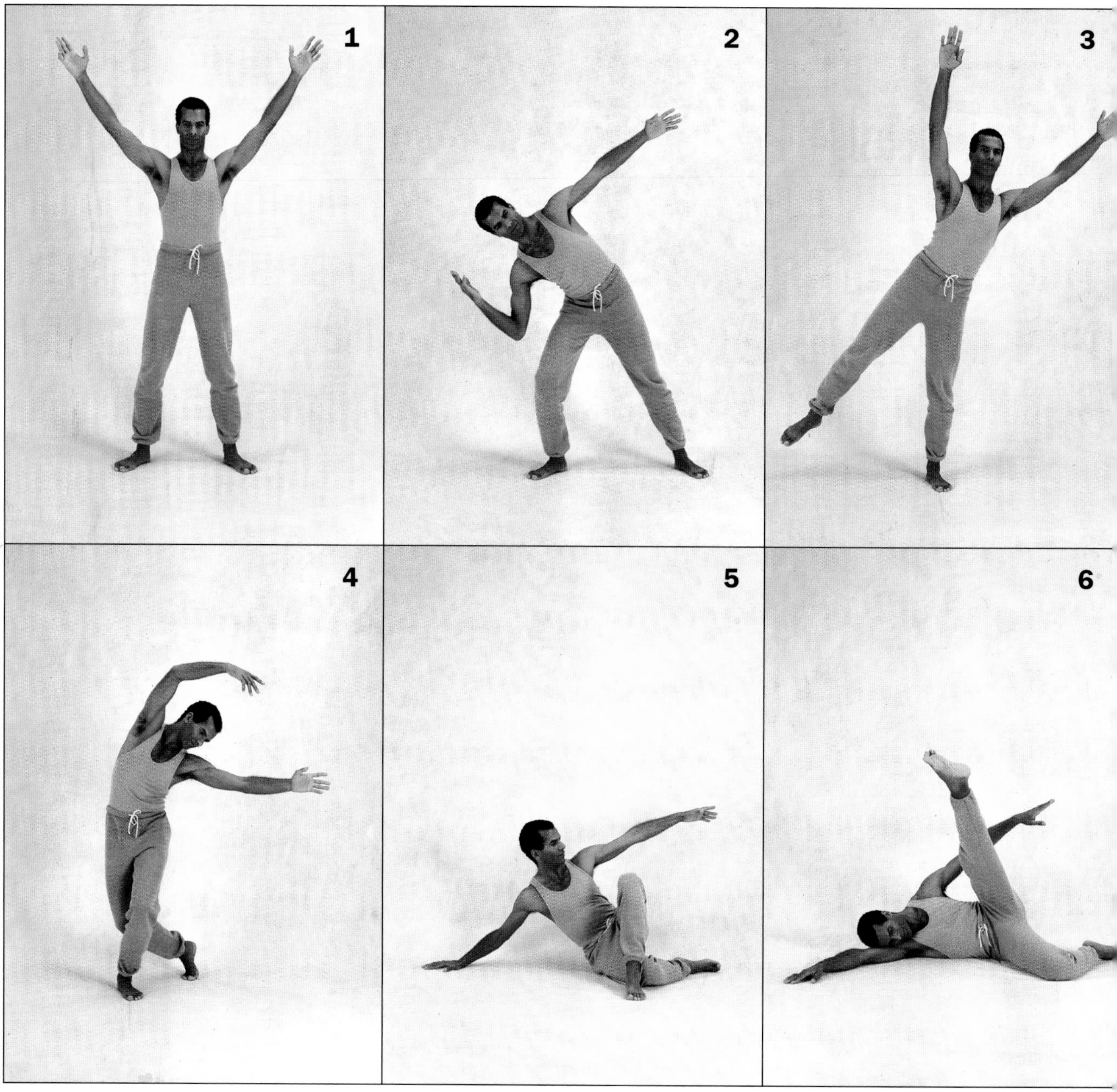

Stand with your legs apart and your arms outstretched (1). Bend your right elbow and bring it down to your bent right knee (2). Extend both arms as you push off with your right foot, shift your weight and lean to the left (3). Bring your bent right leg behind your left leg (4). Lean back to your right and slide down on to your right side (5). Stretch out on your right side as you raise your left leg (6), then lower it and use the momentum to rise on to your right knee (7). Continue to propel yourself forwards to a stand (8).

7

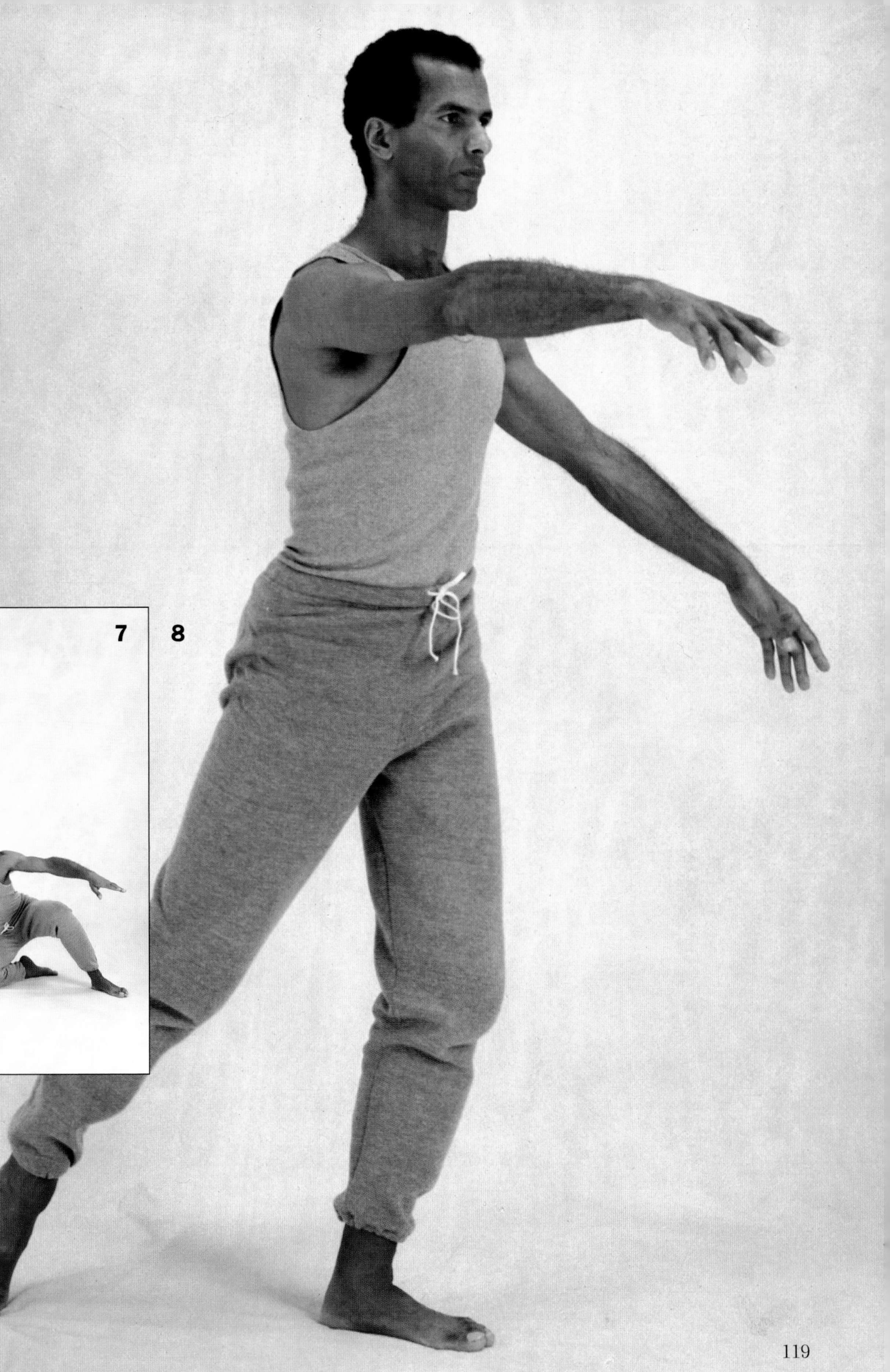

8

Walk-Around

Stand with your feet apart and raise your arms above your head (1). Lower your arms and drop into a crouching position (2), then thrust your body forwards, supporting yourself on your outstretched arms (3). Twist at your waist so your feet are in contact with the floor and take small steps forwards (4), bringing your right arm behind you and your legs in front of you in a "table" position (5). Bend at the hip joint and take small steps backwards to "walk" your legs underneath you, returning to a crouching position (6). Keep your hands on the floor as you straighten your legs as far as you can (7).

1

2

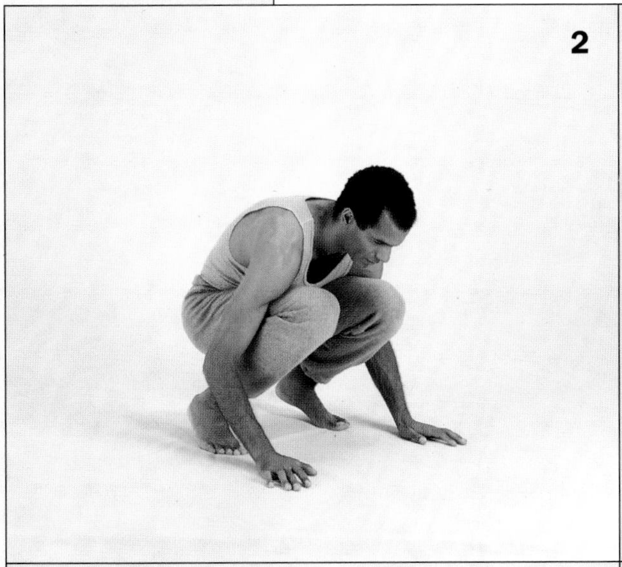

3

4

5

6

7

1

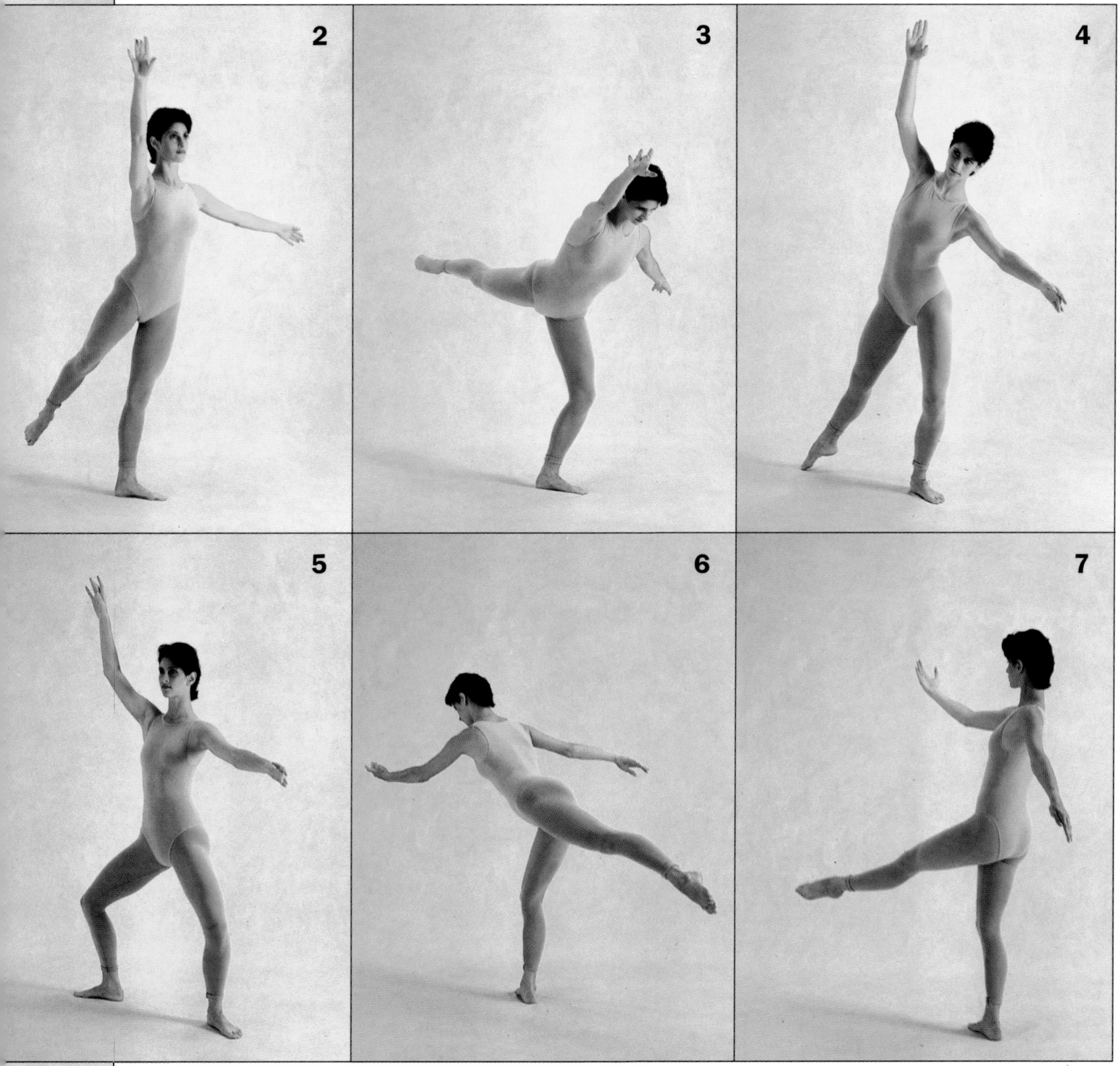

Cantilever

Lean slightly backwards with your left knee bent, your right foot raised in front of you and your arms outstretched (1). Shift your weight and lean forwards as you swing your right leg back (2) and right arm forwards (3). Raise your torso and turn to the right, touching your right foot to the floor (4), then distribute your weight evenly between your legs in a plié position (5). Shift your weight on to your right leg, bringing your left leg back and left arm forwards (6). Swing your left leg and right arm forwards (7).

CHAPTER FIVE

Vitamins A, D, E and K

Micronutrients for bones, muscles and nerves

When you undertake a low-impact exercise programme to reduce the risk of injury to your bones, tendons and ligaments, a diet with sufficient fat-soluble vitamins can complement your programme. The fat-soluble vitamins — A, D, E and K — are needed in small amounts (as are all vitamins) for a variety of functions, one of which is contributing to the growth and strength of your bones. In contrast to the water-soluble B complex and C vitamins, which are used or excreted soon after ingestion and can be stored only in minute quantities, fat-soluble vitamins can be stored in the body wherever fat is deposited. However, because these vitamins are essential to so many physiological processes, they should be included in your diet frequently. The box given on the following page indicates the recommended daily amounts.

Researchers have identified several important functions of vitamin A, including assisting in the growth of bone tissue and of strong tooth enamel, one of the best natural shields against tooth decay. This vitamin also aids in the division and growth of body cells, helps maintain normal vision in dim light and protects the skin and the lining of the nose and throat from infection. In addition, some research indicates that people whose diets include plenty of vegetables that supply vitamin A have a lower incidence of certain forms of cancer, including skin cancer, than people who consume less of these foods.

The vegetables that provide you with vitamin A do so through chemicals called carotenoids — vitamin A precursors that your body converts to vitamin A. The most abundant carotenoid is beta carotene, found in such vegetables and fruits as spinach, broccoli, sweet potatoes, carrots, pumpkin, tomatoes, apricots and peaches. Vitamin A itself is found in generous amounts in egg yolks, dairy products, oily fish and liver — and it occurs not as a precursor, but in a form called retinol that your body uses directly. This does not mean, however, that these animal-derived foods are the best sources of vitamin A. A vegetarian dish such as the Rosy Ratatouille on page 131 and a meat recipe such as the Chopped Liver Spread on page 141 both provide the recommended daily amount.

Animal-derived vitamin A is used in vitamin supplements, but anyone taking supplements should be careful. Doses that exceed 10 times the daily recommended amount can be toxic, potentially causing tenderness or pain in bones as well as liver and brain damage. Beta carotene and other carotenoids, however, are not known to be toxic when you consume more than you need.

Vitamin D can be obtained from your diet, but it is also formed in your skin when you are exposed to sunlight. The regulation of calcium and phosphorus metabolism is vitamin D's most important role. It promotes the intestinal absorption of calcium, regulates the movement of calcium and phosphorus in and out of bones and teeth, and maintains the proper levels of these two minerals in the blood. By promoting an adequate blood level of calcium, vitamin D also ensures the proper functioning of the nerves and muscles.

Vitamin D occurs naturally in only a few common foodstuffs such as oily fish, liver, eggs and butter, however, some milks and many breakfast cereals are fortified with this vitamin. In this chapter, the recipes for Old Fashioned Oat Waffles on page 130, Apricot and Prune Flans on page 137, the Carrot Rice Pudding on page 138 and the Scandinavian-Style Canapés on page 140 contain ample amounts of vitamin D. No one should take vitamin D supplements without medical supervision, since doses that contain more than 10 times the daily recommended amount are extremely toxic.

In contrast to vitamins A and D, vitamin E's functions are not well delineated, although many health and cosmetic claims have been made for it. What is known is that vitamin E acts as an antioxidant, a substance that keeps oxygen from combining with and altering fats. When the fats that are contained in cell membranes react with oxygen, they break down into chemicals called peroxides, and, consequently, the cell membranes are destroyed.

Because of its antioxidant function, some researchers believe that vitamin E may play an important role in inhibiting the long-term

RECOMMENDED DAILY AMOUNTS

Vitamin A is given in retinol equivalents (RE), which measure the vitamin A that you actually absorb, whether you consume retinol (the usable form of vitamin A from animal sources) or beta carotene (the vitamin A precursor from plant foods that your body converts to retinol). One RE is equal to 1 milligram of retinol or 6 milligrams of beta carotene. The Recommended Daily Amount (RDA) is 800 RE for women and 1,000 for men — amounts that are supplied by one large carrot.

Vitamin D is measured in micrograms. The RDA for both men and women is 2.5 micrograms, which can be supplied by 35 grams of sardines.

Vitamin E, which exists in several slightly different chemical forms, is measured in tocopherol equivalents (TE); tocopherol is another name for the vitamin. One milligram of vitamin E equals one TE. There is no British RDA, but an estimated safe intake is 8 to 10 TE, which is supplied by 15 grams of corn oil.

No RDA has been determined for vitamin K either. The suggested intake is 70 to 140 micrograms per day, the amount contained in 50 grams of spinach.

The Basic Guidelines

For a moderately active adult, Britain's National Advisory Committee on Nutrition Education recommends a diet that is low in fat, high in carbohydrates and moderate in protein. The committee's proposals for the long term suggest that no more than 30 per cent of your calories come from fat, that around 11 per cent come from protein and hence that 55 to 60 per cent come from carbohydrates. A gram of fat equals nine calories, while a gram of protein or carbohydrate equals four calories; therefore, if you eat 2,100 calories a day, you should consume approximately 70 grams of fat, 310 grams of carbohydrate and 60 grams of protein daily. If you follow a low-fat/high-carbohydrate diet, your chance of developing heart disease, cancer and other life-threatening diseases may be considerably reduced.

The nutrition charts that accompany each of the low-fat/high-carbohydrate recipes in this book include the number of calories per serving, the number of grams of fat, carbohydrate and protein in a serving, and the percentage of calories derived from each of these nutrients. In addition, the charts provide the amount of calcium, iron and sodium per serving.

Calcium deficiency may be associated with periodontal diseases — which attack the mouth's bones and tissues, including the gums — in both men and women, and with osteoporosis, or bone shrinking and weakening, in elderly women. The deficiency may also contribute to high blood pressure. The daily allowance for calcium recommended by the United Kingdom Department of Health and Social Security (DHSS) is 500 milligrams a day for men and women. Pregnant and lactating women are advised to consume 1,200 milligrams daily.

Although one way you can reduce your fat intake is to cut your consumption of red meat, you should make sure that you get your necessary iron from other sources. The DHSS suggests a minimum of 10 milligrams of iron per day for men and 12 milligrams for women between the ages of 18 and 54.

High sodium intake is associated with high blood pressure in susceptible people. Most adults should restrict sodium intake to about 2,000 milligrams a day, according to the World Health Organization. One way to keep sodium consumption in check is not to add table salt to food.

cellular deterioration that occurs as part of the ageing process and that may be due to oxidation. As a protector of cell membranes, vitamin E may also keep blood cells from breaking down. Among the good sources of vitamin E are oats, leafy green vegetables, whole-wheat products, nuts and virtually all vegetable oils except coconut oil.

Although your body does not make vitamin K directly, bacteria in your intestines can produce this vitamin, which reduces the amount you need from dietary sources. Used by your liver to make blood-clotting factors, vitamin K is found in spinach, kale, cabbage, cauliflower and liver, among other foods.

Measurable deficiencies of the fat-soluble vitamins are relatively uncommon, but no one who exercises regularly can afford to neglect the foods that contain these vitamins. The recipes that follow in this chapter are high in one or more of them.

Spiced Peach Bread

Breakfast

SPICED PEACH BREAD

This bread supplies nearly half of your daily recommended vitamin A; a serving of a typical wholemeal bread provides less than 2 per cent.

CALORIES per slice	135
79% Carbohydrate	27 g
9% Protein	3 g
12% Fat	2 g
CALCIUM	40 mg
IRON	2 mg
SODIUM	59 mg

200 g (7 oz) cooked acorn, butternut or other winter squash, or 1 small uncooked squash
175 g (6 oz) dried peaches
12.5 cl (4 fl oz) apple juice
300 g (10 oz) plain flour
100 g (3½ oz) sugar
2 teaspoons baking powder
1 teaspoon ground allspice
½ teaspoon salt
¼ teaspoon bicarbonate of soda
2 eggs, beaten
1 tablespoon corn oil

If using uncooked squash, preheat the oven to 190°C (375°F or Mark 5). Using a large, heavy knife, carefully halve the squash. Place the halves cut side down on a foil-lined baking sheet and bake for 25 to 35 minutes, or until the flesh is tender when pierced with a knife. Remove the squash from the oven and set aside to cool; reduce the oven temperature to 180°C (350°F or Mark 4). Meanwhile, coarsely chop the peaches. Bring the apple juice to the boil in a small saucepan over medium heat. Remove the pan from the heat and stir in the peaches; set aside. When the squash is cool enough to handle, remove and discard the seeds and stringy membranes. Measure 200 g (7 oz) of the cooked flesh into a small bowl and mash it with a fork; set aside. Reserve any remaining squash for another use.

Lightly oil a 22 by 12 cm (9 by 5 inch) loaf tin and dust it lightly with flour. In a large bowl, stir together the flour, sugar, baking powder, allspice, salt and bicarbonate of soda, and make a well in the centre. Add the peaches and apple juice, the eggs, oil and mashed squash, and mix just until blended. Turn the batter into the prepared tin and bake for 1¼ hours or until the loaf pulls away from the sides of the tin. Let the bread cool in the tin for 15 minutes, then turn it out on to a rack to cool completely. Cut the bread into sixteen 1 cm (½ inch) thick slices. Makes 16 servings

HOT FRUIT COMPOTE

A serving of this dish gives you about one quarter of your recommended daily vitamin C. The golden-yellow flesh of nectarines and plums comes from their beta carotene, a substance your body converts to vitamin A.

750 g (1½ lb) black grapes, washed and stemmed
1 lemon, cut into wedges
2 teaspoons pure vanilla extract
2 Granny Smith apples
2 nectarines
2 plums

Purée the grapes in a food processor or blender. Strain the purée into a medium-sized bowl, pressing with a rubber spatula to extract as much juice as possible; you should have about 25 cl (8 fl oz). Discard the pulp and seeds. Place the juice in a medium-sized non-reactive saucepan, add the lemon and vanilla extract and bring to the boil. Meanwhile, core the apples and stone the nectarines and plums; do not peel the fruit. Cut the fruit into 1 cm (½ inch) thick wedges and add it to the pan. Cover the pan, reduce the heat and simmer, stirring occasionally, for 10 to 15 minutes, or until the fruit is tender. Serve the compote hot, or cover and refrigerate it and serve it chilled. It will keep for four days in the refrigerator. Makes 4 servings

CALORIES per serving	130
90% Carbohydrate	32 g
4% Protein	1 g
6% Fat	1 g
CALCIUM	16 mg
IRON	Trace
SODIUM	1 mg

CUCUMBER COOLER

The banana in this refreshing drink contains beta carotene, which recent studies have shown may protect against some types of cancer.

25 cl (8 fl oz) buttermilk
One 5 cm (2 inch) cucumber section, peeled and cut into large chunks
1 banana
4 mint sprigs
1 ice cube

Combine all the ingredients in a food processor or blender and process until well blended. Pour the cooler into a tall glass and serve. Makes 1 serving

CALORIES per serving	215
72% Carbohydrate	41 g
17% Protein	10 g
11% Fat	3 g
CALCIUM	307 mg
IRON	1 mg
SODIUM	260 mg

OLD-FASHIONED OAT WAFFLES

CALORIES per serving	435
58% Carbohydrate	63 g
16% Protein	18 g
26% Fat	12 g
CALCIUM	336 mg
IRON	3 mg
SODIUM	517 mg

Since your body needs sunshine to synthesize vitamin D, you may need more dietary sources of this vitamin in winter, when you probably get less sunshine. The eggs in these waffles are a source of vitamin D, and you also get a substantial amount of oats, with their cholesterol-lowering fibre.

25 cl (8 fl oz) plain low-fat yogurt
250 g (8 oz) unsweetened apple sauce
1 teaspoon pure vanilla extract
1¼ teaspoons ground cinnamon
125 g (4 oz) plain flour
160 g (5½ oz) rolled oats
2 teaspoons baking powder
2 eggs, separated
¼ teaspoon salt
25 cl (8 fl oz) skimmed milk
30 g (1 oz) butter, melted and cooled

For the sauce, stir together the yogurt, apple sauce, vanilla extract and 1 teaspoon of the cinnamon in a small bowl; set aside. In a medium-sized bowl, stir together the flour, oats and baking powder; set aside. In a large bowl, beat the egg whites until frothy, using an electric mixer. Add the salt and continue to beat until the whites are stiff but not dry; set aside. Make a well in the centre of the dry ingredients, add the milk, egg yolks and butter, and stir just until combined. Fold in the egg whites.

Preheat a non-stick waffle iron. (If your waffle iron does not have a non-stick surface, lightly oil it before preheating it. Do not re-oil the hot iron.) Pour 5 to 6 tablespoons of batter into the centre of each section of the waffle iron and cook the waffles for about 4 minutes, or according to the manufacturer's instructions, until they are golden. Make eight more individual waffles (filling the iron twice) in the same fashion. Divide the 12 individual waffles among four plates, top them with the yogurt sauce and dust them with the remaining cinnamon.

Makes 4 servings

TOMATO-LEMON BREAKFAST SHAKE

CALORIES per serving	265
66% Carbohydrate	45 g
21% Protein	14 g
13% Fat	4 g
CALCIUM	484 mg
IRON	2 mg
SODIUM	453 mg

Carotene is the provitamin, or precursor, of vitamin A that gives carrots their orange hue. The vitamin A content of carrots increases while they are in storage as long as they are kept in a cool, dark place.

1 large carrot
25 cl (8 fl oz) plain low-fat yogurt
1 tablespoon sugar
150 g (5 oz) drained canned tomatoes
1 teaspoon grated lemon rind

Trim and peel the carrot and cut it into 1 cm (½ inch) chunks. Place the carrot in a small saucepan with 25 cl (8 fl oz) of water and bring to the boil over high heat. Reduce the heat to low and simmer, partially covered, for 5 minutes. Drain the carrot and cool it in the refrigerator for about 15 minutes.

Place the carrot in a food processor or blender and process until it is smoothly puréed. Add the yogurt, sugar, tomatoes and lemon rind and process for 1 minute, or until smooth, scraping down the sides of the container with a rubber spatula if necessary. Pour the shake into a tall glass, over ice if desired, and serve.

Makes 1 serving

Lunch

ROSY RATATOUILLE

This version of a classic Provençal dish is rich in vitamins A and C.

CALORIES per serving	260
73% Carbohydrate	46 g
11% Protein	7 g
16% Fat	5 g
CALCIUM	151 mg
IRON	4 mg
SODIUM	407 mg

500 g (1 lb) orange-fleshed sweet potatoes
350 g (12 oz) baby beetroots
350 g (12 oz) carrots
350 g (12 oz) yellow courgettes
1 tablespoon safflower oil
500 g (1 lb) onions, chopped
4 garlic cloves, crushed
850 g (28 oz) canned plum tomatoes, with their liquid
¼ teaspoon dried basil
¼ teaspoon dried thyme
1 bay leaf
4 tablespoons chopped parsley

Wash and trim the vegetables; peel all except the courgettes. Cut the sweet potatoes, beetroots and courgettes into 5 mm (¼ inch) thick slices and halve the larger slices crosswise. Cut the carrots into 2.5 cm (1 inch) chunks.

Heat the oil in a fireproof casserole over medium heat. Add the onions and garlic and cook, stirring, for 10 minutes, or until the onions are soft. Add the sweet potatoes, tomatoes with their liquid, basil, thyme and bay leaf; bring to the boil. Cover, reduce the heat and simmer for 15 to 20 minutes, until the potatoes are tender. Add the beetroots, carrots and parsley, and simmer for 15 minutes. Add the courgettes, increase the heat and cook, uncovered, for 5 minutes, or until the liquid is thickened. Remove and discard the bay leaf. Serve warm, or refrigerate for 3 hours and serve cold. Makes 4 servings

Note: steam mature beetroots whole for about 30 minutes, or until barely tender, then cool slightly, peel, slice and add them to the ratatouille.

Rosy Ratatouille

CREAMY SWEETCORN AND OAT SOUP

CALORIES per serving	155
73% Carbohydrate	30 g
15% Protein	6 g
12% Fat	2 g
CALCIUM	22 mg
IRON	1 mg
SODIUM	47 mg

Most grains lose up to 80 per cent of their vitamin E when the bran and germ are removed in milling. When oats are milled, however, only the inedible hull is removed, so the oats remain a good source of vitamin E, thiamine and fibre.

325 g (11 oz) fresh or frozen sweetcorn kernels
90 g (3 oz) rolled oats
90 g (3 oz) onion, chopped
2 garlic cloves, crushed
¼ teaspoon pepper
Pinch of salt
2 tablespoons chopped parsley

In a medium-sized saucepan, combine the sweetcorn, oats, onion, garlic, pepper, salt and 90 cl (1½ pints) of water. Bring the mixture to the boil over medium heat, reduce the heat to low and simmer for 15 minutes. If a thinner soup is preferred, add a little more water. Remove the pan from the heat, stir in half of the parsley and divide the soup among four bowls. Sprinkle the soup with the remaining parsley and serve. Makes 4 servings

BUTTERNUT SQUASH SANDWICH

Almonds and peanuts, rich sources of vitamin E, should be eaten in moderation because of their high fat content. Here, a sandwich spread made with peanut butter and almonds complements butternut squash.

CALORIES per serving	260
58% Carbohydrate	41 g
17% Protein	12 g
25% Fat	8 g
CALCIUM	168 mg
IRON	3 mg
SODIUM	423 mg

1 small butternut squash
4 whole blanched almonds
4 tablespoons plain low-fat yogurt
2 teaspoons peanut butter
1 spring onion, trimmed and chopped
Pinch of salt
Four 1 cm (½ inch) thick slices dense wholemeal bread
2 large lettuce leaves, torn into bite-sized pieces
1 small tomato, sliced
30 g (1 oz) alfalfa sprouts

Preheat the oven to 190°C (375°F or Mark 5). Line a baking sheet with aluminium foil. Using a large, heavy knife, carefully halve the squash. Place the squash halves cut side down on the baking sheet and bake for 25 minutes, or until the flesh is tender when pierced with a knife. Remove the squash from the oven and set aside to cool. Meanwhile, place the almonds in a small frying pan and toast them over medium-high heat for 2 to 3 minutes, or until golden, tossing them frequently to prevent scorching. For the dressing, place the almonds in a food processor or blender (if using a blender, first coarsely chop the almonds) and process until ground. Add the yogurt, peanut butter, spring onion and salt, and process until blended; set aside.

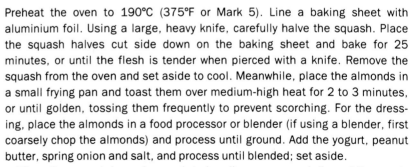

When the squash is cool enough to handle, remove and discard the seeds and stringy membranes. Peel one squash half and cut it lengthwise into four 5 mm (¼ inch) thick slices. (The remaining squash can be used in Spiced Peach Bread, page 128.) Dip the squash slices in the dressing and set aside. Toast the bread and spread each piece with 1 tablespoon of dressing. Layer the lettuce, tomato, squash and sprouts on two pieces of toast and top with the remaining dressing. Place a second slice of toast on each sandwich, cut the sandwiches in half and serve immediately. Makes 2 servings

BROCCOLI PIMIENTO SALAD

Dark green vegetables are rich sources of carotene: the broccoli in a serving of this salad supplies more than one fifth of your daily requirement of vitamin A. Broccoli is also a good source of calcium. The wholemeal bread and corn oil contribute vitamin E to this dish.

CALORIES per serving	110
58% Carbohydrate	17 g
16% Protein	5 g
26% Fat	4 g
CALCIUM	61 mg
IRON	2 mg
SODIUM	206 mg

500 g (1 lb) broccoli
4 slices wholemeal bread, cut into 1 cm (½ inch) cubes
3 whole canned pimientos
4 tablespoons balsamic vinegar
2 teaspoons corn oil
2 teaspoons grainy Dijon mustard
1 garlic clove, crushed
¼ teaspoon dried tarragon
¼ teaspoon pepper
Pinch of salt

Preheat the oven to 190°C (375°F or Mark 5). Wash and trim the broccoli. Cut off the florets and cut the stems into 2.5 cm (1 inch) pieces; set aside. For the croutons, spread the bread cubes on a baking sheet and bake them for 5 to 10 minutes, or until golden. Meanwhile, bring 50 cl (16 fl oz) of water to the boil in a large saucepan over medium-high heat. Add the broccoli florets and stems and cook for 5 minutes, or until the stems are tender when pierced with a knife. Drain the broccoli, cool under cold running water and set aside to drain thoroughly. Rinse and pat dry the pimientos and cut them into 5 mm (¼ inch) wide strips; set aside.

For the dressing, whisk together the vinegar, oil, mustard, garlic, tarragon, pepper, salt and 2 tablespoons of water in a small bowl. Pat the broccoli dry, then place it in a large bowl with the pimiento. Add the croutons, pour on the dressing and toss to combine. Serve the salad immediately so that the croutons remain crisp.

Makes 4 servings

INDIAN SPICED PUMPKIN SOUP

If you eat pumpkin only rarely you miss out on an excellent source of vitamin A. You can also toast and eat the pumpkin seeds, an abundant source of vitamin E. A 1 kg (2 lb) pumpkin will yield the quantity of cooked pumpkin used here.

2 teaspoons butter
125 g (4 oz) onion, coarsely chopped
1 teaspoon ground coriander
½ teaspoon ground cumin
½ teaspoon ground turmeric
500 g (1 lb) cooked pumpkin
4 tablespoons chopped fresh coriander
2 tablespoons brown sugar
2 tablespoons tomato paste
1 tablespoon peanut butter
¼ teaspoon pepper
Pinch of salt

Melt the butter in a medium-sized saucepan over medium heat. Add the onion and sauté for 3 to 4 minutes, or until light golden. Add the ground coriander, cumin and turmeric, and cook, stirring, for another minute. Add the pumpkin, fresh coriander, sugar, tomato paste, peanut butter, pepper, salt and 75 cl (1¼ pints) of water, and stir gently to mix well. Bring the mixture to the boil, then cover the pan, reduce the heat to low and simmer the soup for about 30 minutes, or until the flavours are well blended. Ladle the soup into four bowls and serve.

Makes 4 servings

CALORIES per serving	130
61% Carbohydrate	21 g
10% Protein	3 g
29% Fat	5 g
CALCIUM	55 mg
IRON	3 mg
SODIUM	146 mg

Dinner

RICE-STUFFED ROASTED POUSSINS WITH KALE

CALORIES per serving	360
50% Carbohydrate	44 g
28% Protein	25 g
22% Fat	9 g
CALCIUM	120 mg
IRON	3 mg
SODIUM	114 mg

In this recipe, the sweetcorn and the brown rice — a whole grain — contribute vitamin E and several B vitamins, as well as fibre.

15 g (½ oz) butter
45 g (1½ oz) spring onions, chopped
3 garlic cloves, chopped
250 g (8 oz) cooked brown rice
175 g (6 oz) frozen sweetcorn kernels, thawed
175 g (6 oz) cooked couscous
1 tablespoon chopped fresh rosemary
2 poussins (about 350 g/12 oz each)
2 onions
250 g (8 oz) kale

Preheat the oven to 220°C (425°F or Mark 7). For the stuffing, heat the butter in a small frying pan over medium heat. Add the spring onions and garlic and sauté for 3 minutes, then transfer to a medium-sized bowl, add the rice, sweetcorn, couscous and rosemary and mix well.

Remove and discard any visible fat from the poussins, then stuff them. Place any extra stuffing in a small baking dish and cover with foil. Line a roasting pan with foil. Peel the onions, slice them 5 mm (¼ inch) thick and spread them in the pan. Place the poussins on top and roast for 15 minutes, basting with the pan juices. Meanwhile, wash and trim the kale. Add 17.5 cl (6 fl oz) of water to the roasting pan, reduce the heat to 180°C (350°F or Mark 4) and place the dish of stuffing in the oven. Cook the stuffing and the poussins for 30 minutes, or until the juices run clear when the thigh joints are pierced.

Remove the dish of stuffing from the oven and keep it warm. Transfer the

Rice-Stuffed Roasted Poussins with Kale

poussins to a platter and cover with foil. Scrape the onions and pan juices into a medium-sized saucepan and bring to the boil. Add the kale and cover the pan. Reduce the heat to medium low and simmer the kale, stirring occasionally, for 10 minutes, or until tender. Divide the stuffing and kale among four plates. Split the poussins, place one half on each plate and serve. Remove the skin from the poussins before eating. Makes 4 servings

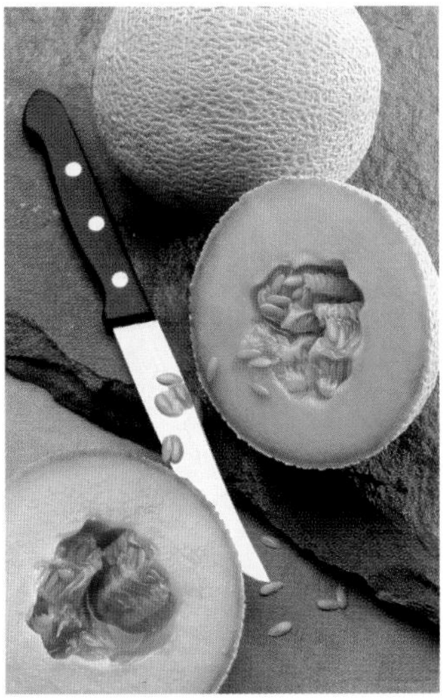

SUMMER MELON SOUP

Puréed sweet potato, not cream, thickens this soup which is rich in vitamins A and C.

2 cantaloupe melons
500 g (1 lb) orange-fleshed sweet potatoes, trimmed
25 cl (8 fl oz) skimmed milk
25 cl (8 fl oz) plain low-fat yogurt
4 tablespoons apple juice concentrate
1 tablespoon grated lemon rind
8 mint sprigs

Halve and seed the melons. Spoon the flesh into a food processor or blender, process until liquefied and transfer to a large bowl; set aside. Place the sweet potatoes in a medium-sized saucepan with cold water to cover and bring to the boil. Reduce the heat, partially cover the pan and simmer for 45 minutes, or until the sweet potatoes are tender; drain and set aside to cool.

When the sweet potatoes are cool enough to handle, peel them, cut them into large chunks and process until puréed. Gradually add the melon juice, the milk, yogurt, apple juice concentrate and lemon rind, and process until well blended. Return the soup to the bowl and add four of the mint sprigs, crushing them gently to release their flavour. Cover the bowl and refrigerate the soup overnight. To serve, remove the mint, ladle the soup into four bowls and garnish with the remaining mint. Makes 4 servings

CALORIES per serving	270
81% Carbohydrate	57 g
13% Protein	9 g
6% Fat	2 g
CALCIUM	233 mg
IRON	1 mg
SODIUM	111 mg

CAVIARE-OLIVE PASTA SALAD

Parsley is rich in both beta carotene and vitamin E.

175 g (6 oz) fusilli (spiral pasta)
100 g (3½ oz) low-fat cottage cheese (1% fat)
30 g (1 oz) parsley sprigs
2 tablespoons coarsely chopped spring onions
4 tablespoons skimmed milk
Pinch of pepper
8 large stoned black olives, slivered
1 teaspoon red caviare

Bring a large pan of water to the boil, add the pasta and cook for 10 minutes, or according to the packet directions until *al dente.* Drain the pasta, cool under cold water and set aside to drain thoroughly. For the sauce, process the cottage cheese, parsley and spring onions in a food processor or blender for 1 to 2 minutes, or until smooth, scraping down the sides of the container with a rubber spatula as necessary. Add the milk and pepper and process for another 5 seconds. Transfer the pasta and sauce to a large bowl and toss to coat the pasta with the sauce. Scatter the olives and caviare on top and toss the salad again just before serving. Makes 4 servings

CALORIES per serving	200
69% Carbohydrate	34 g
19% Protein	9 g
12% Fat	3 g
CALCIUM	57 mg
IRON	2 mg
SODIUM	107 mg

WILD RICE SALAD WITH WALNUT-ORANGE DRESSING

CALORIES per serving	245
59% Carbohydrate	38 g
14% Protein	9 g
27% Fat	8 g
CALCIUM	35 mg
IRON	3 mg
SODIUM	45 mg

Cooking oils are the richest dietary sources of vitamin E. Brussels sprouts contain some vitamins A and E and are rich in vitamin K.

150 g (5 oz) wild rice
300 g (10 oz) Brussels sprouts, cooked
5 tablespoons freshly squeezed orange juice
2 tablespoons walnut oil
½ teaspoon orange extract
¼ teaspoon pepper
Pinch of salt
100 g (3½ oz) sweet red pepper, slivered
2 tablespoons chopped fresh mint
4 large cos lettuce leaves

Bring 90 cl (1½ pints) of water to the boil in a medium-sized saucepan over medium-high heat. Add the rice, reduce the heat to low and simmer, partially covered, for 45 minutes. Halve the sprouts and set aside.

Remove the pan of rice from the heat and stir in the orange juice, oil, orange extract, pepper and salt. Stir in the Brussels sprouts, red pepper and mint. Let the mixture cool slightly, then transfer it to a large bowl, cover with plastic film and refrigerate it overnight, stirring occasionally. To serve, line a platter with the lettuce leaves and mound the salad on top. Makes 4 servings

GREEN TAMALE PIE

In this recipe, vitamin E comes from several ingredients, including the sweet green pepper, sweetcorn kernels and Cheddar cheese.

325 g (11 oz) frozen broad beans, thawed
60 g (2 oz) washed trimmed spinach
2 spring onions, trimmed and coarsely chopped
2 tablespoons tomato paste
1 garlic clove
4 teaspoons chili powder
90 g (3 oz) sweetcorn kernels
150 g (5 oz) sweet green pepper, coarsely chopped
200 g (7 oz) cornmeal
Pinch of salt
30 g (1 oz) Cheddar cheese, grated

Place the beans, spinach, spring onions, tomato paste, garlic and half the chili powder in a food processor or blender and process for 1 to 2 minutes, or until puréed, scraping down the sides of the container with a rubber spatula as necessary. Stir in the sweetcorn and green pepper and set aside.

Preheat the oven to 180°C (350°F or Mark 4). Lightly oil a shallow, round fireproof casserole or cast iron frying pan with an ovenproof handle; set aside. In a medium-sized saucepan set over medium heat, combine the cornmeal, salt, remaining chili powder and 60 cl (1 pint) of cold water and cook, stirring constantly, for 2 to 3 minutes, or until the mixture thickens and comes to the boil. Remove the pan from the heat and spread two thirds of the cornmeal mixture in the prepared casserole. Spoon the bean purée over it, top with the remaining cornmeal mixture and sprinkle the pie with the cheese. Bake the tamale pie for 30 minutes, or until the cheese is melted and the top is lightly browned. To serve, cut the pie into six wedges. Makes 6 servings

CALORIES per serving	230
75% Carbohydrate	43 g
14% Protein	8 g
11% Fat	3 g
CALCIUM	64 mg
IRON	3 mg
SODIUM	148 mg

Desserts

APRICOT AND PRUNE FLANS

Using eggs and milk together gives you both calcium and vitamin D, which work in tandem to keep your bones strong and healthy. Apricots and prunes, excellent sources of vitamin A, also provide potassium, an important mineral for maintaining body-fluid balance.

CALORIES per serving	245
81% Carbohydrate	52 g
11% Protein	7 g
8% Fat	2 g
CALCIUM	118 mg
IRON	2 mg
SODIUM	64 mg

100 g (3½ oz) dried apricot halves
135 g (4½ oz) stoned prunes
2 eggs
125 g (4 oz) honey
100 g (3½ oz) plain flour
40 cl (14 fl oz) skimmed milk

Place the apricots and prunes in a medium-sized bowl, add boiling water to cover and set aside to soak for 1 hour.

Preheat the oven to 180°C (350°F or Mark 4). For the custard, beat the eggs and honey together in a small bowl until smooth. Gradually whisk in the flour, then stir in the milk. Drain the fruit and divide it among six 25 cl (8 fl oz) ramekins. Divide the custard among the ramekins and bake for 1 hour, or until the custard is set and golden brown round the edges. Serve the flans warm, or cover them, refrigerate until well chilled and serve cold. Makes 6 servings

Apricot and Prune Flans

CHERRY-ALMOND SOUP

Cherries provide some carotene, which the body converts into vitamin A.

CALORIES per serving	60
74% Carbohydrate	12 g
17% Protein	2 g
9% Fat	1 g
CALCIUM	21 mg
IRON	Trace
SODIUM	70 mg

8 almond-flavoured tea bags
2 teaspoons pure vanilla extract
1 tablespoon honey
300 g (10 oz) stoned fresh sweet cherries, or frozen unsweetened cherries
4 tablespoons quark

Bring 1 litre (1¾ pints) of water to the boil. Place the tea bags in a heatproof bowl, pour the boiling water over them, cover and leave to steep for 15 minutes. Remove and discard the tea bags and stir in the vanilla extract and honey; set aside. Place the cherries in a food processor or blender and process until puréed, then stir the cherry purée into the tea. Cover the bowl and refrigerate the soup for at least 4 hours, or until thoroughly chilled. To serve, divide the soup among four bowls and top each serving with 1 tablespoon of the quark. Makes 4 servings

CARROT RICE PUDDING

This traditional dish fulfils your daily requirement for vitamin A while also providing some vitamins D and E.

Calories per serving	260
77% Carbohydrate	51 g
11% Protein	7 g
12% Fat	3 g
CALCIUM	120 mg
IRON	1 mg
SODIUM	91 mg

25 cl (8 fl oz) carrot juice
25 cl (8 fl oz) skimmed milk
4 tablespoons sugar
3 tablespoons instant tapioca
2 eggs, beaten
150 g (5 oz) cooked brown rice (60 g/2 oz raw)
60 g (2 oz) carrot, grated
75 g (2½ oz) raisins

Bring a few centimetres of water to a simmer in the bottom of a double boiler. For the custard, stir the carrot juice, milk, sugar, tapioca and eggs together in the top pan until well blended, then cook, without stirring, over the simmering water for 5 minutes. Increase the heat to medium high to bring the water in the bottom pan to the boil, and cook the custard, whisking constantly, for another 5 minutes. Remove the top pan from the heat and stir the rice, carrot and raisins into the custard. Turn the mixture into a serving dish and leave to cool at room temperature for about 1 hour, or cover and refrigerate for 2 to 3 hours and serve cold. Makes 4 servings

MANDARIN ORANGE WHIP

Evaporated skimmed milk that is fortified with vitamins A and D is rich-tasting but contains less than 1 gram of fat per cup.

CALORIES per serving	200
81% Carbohydrate	42 g
18% Protein	10 g
1% Fat	0.2 g
CALCIUM	224 mg
IRON	1 mg
SODIUM	116 mg

1 kg (2 lb) drained canned mandarin orange segments
3 tablespoons brown sugar
7 g (¼ oz) powdered gelatine
2 teaspoons lime juice
1 teaspoon grated lime rind
25 cl (8 fl oz) fortified evaporated skimmed milk
1 teaspoon pure vanilla extract
2 egg whites

Place half the mandarin oranges in a food processor or blender and process until liquefied, then transfer to a small saucepan and heat over medium-low heat for 5 minutes, or just until tepid. Add the sugar and gelatine, and stir until the gelatine dissolves. Remove the pan from the heat. Add the remaining oranges, the lime juice, lime rind, milk and vanilla extract, and stir to combine.

In a large bowl, beat the egg whites until stiff but not dry, using an electric mixer. Fold the whites into the orange mixture until mixed. Transfer the mixture to a 1.5 litre (2½ pint) soufflé dish or divide it among four individual bowls. Cover and refrigerate for 3 to 4 hours, or until set. Makes 4 servings

MOROCCAN-STYLE FRUITED COUSCOUS

Couscous, a granular semolina product, is usually cooked with meat and vegetables but, like rice, also makes a good dessert. Yogurt adds calcium, and the almonds are a good source of vitamin E.

CALORIES per serving	215
70% Carbohydrate	37 g
19% Protein	6 g
11% Fat	4 g
CALCIUM	89 mg
IRON	1 mg
SODIUM	26 mg

75 g (2½ oz) sultanas
12 whole toasted almonds
5 dried apricot halves, slivered
25 cl (8 fl oz) apple juice
60 g (2 oz) couscous
12.5 cl (4 fl oz) plain low-fat yogurt
1 tablespoon brown sugar
½ teaspoon almond extract

In a small bowl, toss together the sultanas, almonds and apricots. Bring the apple juice to the boil in a medium-sized saucepan over medium heat. Stir in the couscous and cook, stirring, for 2 minutes, or until thickened. Remove the pan from the heat and cover with a tightly fitting lid; set aside for 7 minutes. Stir in the yogurt, sugar and almond extract. Divide the couscous among four bowls and top it with the fruit mixture. Makes 4 servings

CARROT-APPLE SAUCE SQUARES

Egg yolks, unlike other foods, do not reveal their vitamin A content by the intensity of their colour: a pale yolk has as much vitamin A as a dark yellow one. The yolk also contains all the egg's vitamin D.

175 g (6 oz) plain flour
60 g (2 oz) brown sugar
2 teaspoons baking powder
½ teaspoon ground cinnamon
2 eggs
3 tablespoons walnut oil
125 g (4 oz) unsweetened apple sauce
150 g (5 oz) cooked brown rice (60 g/2 oz raw)
125 g (4 oz) carrots, grated

Preheat the oven to 200°C (400°F or Mark 6). Lightly oil a 20 cm (8 inch) square baking tin and lightly flour it; set aside. In a medium-sized bowl, stir together the flour, sugar, baking powder and cinnamon and make a well in the centre. In a small bowl, beat together the eggs, oil and apple sauce. Pour this mixture into the dry ingredients, add the rice and carrots and stir until the dry ingredients are moistened. Spread the batter in the tin and bake for 40 minutes, or until the top is lightly browned and a toothpick inserted into the cake comes out dry. (The cake will rise very little.) Let the cake cool in the tin on a rack for 15 minutes, then cut it into nine squares. Makes 9 servings

CALORIES per serving	185
61% Carbohydrate	28 g
8% Protein	4 g
31% Fat	6 g
CALCIUM	69 mg
IRON	1 mg
SODIUM	117 mg

Scandinavian-Style Canapés

Snacks

SCANDINAVIAN-STYLE CANAPÉS

Fish are the only living creatures that can manufacture vitamin D in the absence of ultraviolet light: fatty fish such as salmon and herring are the richest sources of this vitamin.

4 tablespoons plain low-fat yogurt
2 teaspoons Dijon mustard
1 tablespoon chopped fresh dill, plus 16 dill sprigs
16 slices cocktail pumpernickel bread
Sixteen 5 mm (¼ inch) thick cucumber slices
1 sweet red pepper, cut into sixteen 2.5 cm (1 inch) squares
60 g (2 oz) smoked trout, or smoked salmon, cut into 16 pieces

In a small bowl, stir together the yogurt, mustard and chopped dill. Spread the bread with the yogurt mixture. Place a cucumber slice and a red pepper square on each piece of bread and top with a piece of fish and a dill sprig. Arrange the canapés on a platter and serve. If not serving immediately, cover the platter with plastic film and refrigerate. Makes 4 servings

CALORIES per serving	125
61% Carbohydrate	20 g
18% Protein	6 g
21% Fat	3 g
CALCIUM	73 mg
IRON	1 mg
SODIUM	325 mg

CHOPPED LIVER SPREAD

Chicken liver is a good source of all the fat-soluble vitamins, especially vitamin A, which is stored in the liver. When chopped liver is prepared without added butter or chicken fat, it is a relatively low-fat hors-d'oeuvre.

CALORIES per serving	150
54% Carbohydrate	22 g
16% Protein	6 g
30% Fat	5 g
CALCIUM	10 mg
IRON	3 mg
SODIUM	143 mg

175 g (6 oz) chicken livers, washed and trimmed
2 tablespoons chopped shallots
2 tablespoons plain low-fat yogurt
2 teaspoons Dijon mustard
¼ teaspoon pepper
Pinch of salt
48 small low-sodium savoury biscuits

Bring 35 cl (12 fl oz) of water to the boil in a small saucepan over medium-high heat. Add the chicken livers, reduce the heat to medium low, cover the pan and simmer for 5 minutes, stirring occasionally to ensure even cooking. Drain the livers and set aside to cool, then quarter them, place them in a food processor or blender and process for about 30 seconds, or until smooth. Add the shallots, yogurt, mustard, pepper and salt and process for another 30 seconds. Spread 1 teaspoon of liver on each biscuit. Makes 8 servings

STUFFED TOMATOES

The large, yellow-fleshed swede contains twice as much vitamin C, calcium and potassium as its relative the turnip.

1 large swede (about 560 g/18 oz)
250 g (8 oz) onions, chopped
1 tablespoon chopped parsley
4 teaspoons vegetable oil
2 tablespoons tomato paste
¼ teaspoon pepper, or to taste
Pinch of salt
8 fresh tomatoes (about 850 g/ 1¾ lb)

Using a sharp knife, pare a 5 mm (¼ inch) thickness of skin from the swede. Cut the swede into small chunks and grate it in a food processor using the grating blade, or quarter the swede and grate it by hand. Steam the swede in a vegetable steamer over boiling water for 15 to 20 minutes, or just until the raw taste is gone; the swede should still be crisp. Transfer the cooked swede to a large bowl and set aside to cool.

Mix the cooled swede with the onions and parsley. Heat 2 teaspoons of the oil in a medium-sized frying pan over medium-high heat, add the swede mixture and cook, stirring occasionally, for 2 to 3 minutes, or until the vegetables begin to brown. Add the remaining oil and cook, stirring, for another 2 to 3 minutes. Stir in the tomato paste, pepper and salt, remove the pan from the heat and set aside to cool. Meanwhile, cut off and discard 5 mm (¼ inch) from the stem end of each tomato. Carefully scoop out the flesh, leaving a 5 mm (¼ inch) thick shell, and mix the tomato flesh with the swede mixture. Stuff the tomatoes with the filling, mounding it at the top, and serve. Or wrap the tomatoes in plastic film, refrigerate them until well chilled and cut them in half lengthwise to reveal the filling. Makes 4 servings

CALORIES per serving	140
58% Carbohydrate	22 g
10% Protein	4 g
32% Fat	5 g
CALCIUM	80 mg
IRON	2 mg
SODIUM	136 mg

ACKNOWLEDGEMENTS

The Rockport Fitness Walking Test on page 21 was reprinted courtesy of The Rockport Company, © 1987 The Rockport Company.

Nutritional analyses provided by Hill Nutrition Associates, New York State.

The editors wish to thank Kate Cann and Norma MacMillan.

Index prepared by Ian Tucker.

PHOTOGRAPHY CREDITS

Cover photograph by Julian Bajzert, London; exercise photographs by Andrew Eccles; water workouts photographs by John Zimmerman; food photographs by Steven Mays, Rebus, Inc.

ILLUSTRATION CREDITS

Page 9, illustration: David Flaherty; page 10, illustration: Brian Sisco, Tammi Colichio; page 15, illustration: David Flaherty, chart: Brian Sisco; page 16, illustration: Brian Sisco, Tammi Colichio; page 21, chart: Brian Sisco, Tammi Colichio; page 23, illustration: Tammi Colichio; pages 62-63, charts: Brian Sisco, Tammi Colichio.